MYRTLEFIELD

HOUSE

Windows
on Paradise

Windows
on Paradise

Scenes of Hope and Salvation
in Luke's Gospel

David Gooding

Myrtlefield Discoveries

For

Arthur and Anne Williamson

Contents

Preface to the 1976 Edition

A very pleasing feature of life in Ireland during these last ten years (a feature admittedly not so well publicized as some others) has been the remarkable growth of interest in the study of holy Scripture. In numerous groups all over the country ordinary people with no professional training in theology have been discovering that they can find God for themselves through active personal study of the Bible.

It was as a small contribution to the work of certain groups who were at the time engaged on a year-long study of Luke's Gospel that the talks embodied in this little book were originally given. They were intended neither as a general survey of the whole Gospel nor as a detailed exposition of particular passages in it. Their purpose was to encourage the hearers to pursue their own detailed study of the Gospel by first of all engaging their minds and imaginations in a broad study of a few of the Gospel's leading themes.

That the talks were ever given at all was due to the encouragement of Arthur and Anne Williamson. That they now appear in print for a wider public is likewise due to their zeal and hard work in organizing the recording, transcribing, editing and typing of the material. This onerous task is but one example of the multifarious and indefatigable labours which they constantly perform in the cause of encouraging their fellow-countrymen to enjoy their God-given heritage of holy Scripture. It belongs to Another to appraise their work: but I may be allowed on the behalf of the very many who have benefited from their toil to record our admiration and gratitude.

David Gooding
Belfast

Publisher's update

Since this *Preface* was written, *Windows on Paradise* has been translated into nine languages, including: Albanian, Russian, Spanish and Vietnamese. More than 500,000 copies have been sold or given away so far.

Introduction

Luke's record of the life and ministry of Jesus Christ has been called the most artistic of the four Gospels. That may be so, but it certainly is filled with scenes whose rich detail and vivid beauty reveal Christ's character and majesty. These scenes bring before us the Christ of God reaching out to people in their needs, answering their deepest questions and presenting himself as the one to whom they owe their lives and loyalty. Clearly, Luke has chosen events rich with a significance beyond their artistic merit.

In this series of studies we will consider a selection of these scenes, topically grouped into three panoramic views. Each panorama will focus our attention on different aspects of Luke's presentation of Christ.

We will see first how Luke shows Christ to be the champion of the outcast and the oppressed who came to reclaim and restore those with the greatest need. Such incidents might lead us to think that Christ holds out hope for even the most difficult cases. But can such stories really give us hope now? After all, these events occurred centuries ago, and questions about our existence, of death and a life to come seem, for many, unanswered at best and perhaps unknowable. Luke indicates that he is aware of profound questions about time, eternity and death, for he has selected events that show the answers he found in Christ, the one who gives hope both in the here and the hereafter. Indeed, it was in Christ that Luke found someone worthy to rule both his future destiny and his life in the here and now. And he does not let his readers think of the Lord Jesus as a king who is relevant for the next life only. By recounting the way this king relates to his subjects and wins their hearts, he reveals his character and shows the significance of the king and his present kingdom.

After looking at Christ in all these settings, some may be left with questions. Does Luke provide answers only for those who believe already, or also for doubters and sceptics? What about those who have serious doubts about miracles? We will return to the beginning of Luke's Gospel to see how he addresses questions of faith and doubt as they arose at the time of Christ's birth, in the lives of his own family.

To gain as much as possible from these studies, it will be helpful to read the suggested passages from Luke's Gospel that are listed at the start of each chapter. For those who would like to make use of them, questions for reflection and group study are included in a study guide at the end of the book.

The Gospel of the Outcast and Oppressed

Reclaiming *a* Prostitute

One of the Pharisees asked him to eat with him, and he went into the Pharisee's house and took his place at the table. And behold, a woman of the city, who was a sinner, when she learned that he was reclining at table in the Pharisee's house, brought an alabaster flask of ointment, and standing behind him at his feet, weeping, she began to wet his feet with her tears and wiped them with the hair of her head and kissed his feet and anointed them with the ointment.

Now when the Pharisee who had invited him saw this, he said to himself, 'If this man were a prophet, he would have known who and what sort of woman this is who is touching him, for she is a sinner.'

And Jesus answering said to him, 'Simon, I have something to say to you.' And he answered, 'Say it, Teacher.'

'A certain money-lender had two debtors. One owed five hundred denarii, and the other fifty. When they could not pay, he cancelled the debt of both. Now which of them will love him more?'

Simon answered, 'The one, I suppose, for whom he cancelled the larger debt.'

And he said to him, 'You have judged rightly.'

Then turning towards the woman he said to Simon, 'Do you see this woman? I entered your house; you gave me no water for my feet, but she has wet my feet with her tears and wiped them with her hair. You gave me no kiss, but from the time I came in she has not ceased to kiss my feet. You did not anoint my head with oil, but she has anointed my feet with ointment. Therefore I tell you, her sins, which are many, are forgiven—for she loved much. But he who is forgiven little, loves little.'

And he said to her, 'Your sins are forgiven.'

Then those who were at table with him began to say among themselves, 'Who is this, who even forgives sins?'

And he said to the woman, 'Your faith has saved you; go in peace.'

Soon afterwards he went on through cities and villages, proclaiming and bringing the good news of the kingdom of God. And the twelve were with him, and also some women who had been healed of evil spirits and infirmities: Mary, called Magdalene, from whom seven demons had gone out, and Joanna, the wife of Chuza, Herod's household manager, and Susanna, and many others, who provided for them out of their means.

Luke 7:36–8:3

One of the most beautiful features of the Gospel of Luke is the way it depicts Christ as the Champion and Saviour of the outcast and the oppressed, as the one who can restore true human dignity to men and women whom life has somehow warped, or society has rejected or even persecuted. It is the purpose of this series of studies to examine in detail some of the case histories of such people who were reclaimed and restored by Christ.

It has often been observed that the description of Christ as 'a friend of tax collectors and sinners' (Luke 7:34), though intended originally by Christ's enemies as a serious indictment of his integrity, has become in the eyes of Christians one of his greatest glories. But the second term, sinners, is a euphemism, as we can see if we compare Luke's phrase with the similar one in the Gospel of Matthew 21:31, 'the tax collectors and the prostitutes go into the kingdom of God before you'. If, then, instead of the euphemism we use the normal, ugly word and refer to Christ as the 'friend of tax collectors and prostitutes', the phrase no longer seems quite so charming even in Christian ears. Indeed, the pious Christian may well find the phrase offensive. Originally, of course, that was the intention. It was not coined in a permissive society. Those who first used it meant to expose what they considered was an affront to common decency and morality, let alone the strict religious standards of the time; an affront all the more grievous by being offered in the name of God and true religion. They thought Christ was a fraud, and their suspicions were only increased when they observed the kind of women he allowed to follow him on his preaching tours.

There was, for instance, the wife of Chuza, Herod's steward; but Herod's palace was notorious for its loose standards, and anyone who had moved in that unrestrained set was bound to be suspect to the strict religious Jew. And then there was Mary Magdalene, the lowest of the low, 'from whom seven demons had gone out', says Luke (8:2); which, whatever it means, indicates that her past had been evil beyond description. A young, attractive man, leader of a new and unorthodox religious sect, followed by a band of female devotees whose past life had been neurotically immoral—it is not difficult to imagine what the religiously orthodox made of it.

And it would be less than realistic to overlook the reasons why their criticisms would have seemed to them absolutely justified. Like our own world, only more so, the ancient world was well acquainted with religious groups that made religion a thin disguise for sexual perversion. Of course Christ, if questioned, would have maintained that these women had been converted from their evil life, but this is precisely what the Pharisees would have disputed. Indeed, it is likely that they would have denied outright that some sudden conversion experience could have turned these women into suitable company for anyone, let alone a prophet.

Still there was a puzzle. In his public preaching, this Jesus had demanded moral standards higher than anyone previously had ever been known to set, and had openly denounced the Pharisees for not keeping these standards. They were content, he said, with a mere external respectability, while all the time being guilty of an inner spiritual immorality.

> Unless your righteousness exceeds that of the scribes and Pharisees, you will never enter into the kingdom of heaven. . . . You have heard that it was said, 'You shall not commit adultery.' But I say to you that everyone who looks at a woman with lustful intent has already committed adultery with her in his heart. (Matt 5:20, 27–28)

What was one to make of this Jesus? Was he sincere? His teaching would convict the saintliest person of sin. Was he sinless himself? Was he a prophet? What about these questionable characters that were so often to be seen in his company?

It was with such questions in his mind that a Pharisee named Simon invited our Lord to lunch. Conversation at the table would perhaps, so he thought, give him an opportunity to assess Jesus more closely. Presently, as the meal was progressing, the door opened and in glided a woman somewhat self-consciously, and made for the place where Christ was, after the eastern manner, reclining at the table.

At once Simon was annoyed. He knew the woman for one of the notorious characters about town, and such people were not normally allowed in his home. But he was astonished when he saw what happened next. Reaching a point directly behind Christ, she dropped down on the floor at his feet and began quietly to weep. She was so near Christ that, as she wept, some of her tears actually fell on his feet, and—embarrassed—she clutched some of her long flowing hair and tried to wipe the tears off.

Then to Simon's utter amazement she kissed his feet, and finally drew out a small flask and anointed his feet with ointment. It all happened so quickly. Simon's first reaction had been to order his servants to remove the woman at once; but then the woman grasped Christ's feet and Simon hesitated, fully expecting some indignant outburst from Christ. But Christ had said nothing; in fact he had given no indication that he thought anything unusual had happened. And so the meal had gone on.

But the conversation had become disjointed, for Simon was now deep in thought. 'That settles it,' Simon was saying to himself. 'This man is no prophet; for if he were, he would have known who this woman is that is touching him and what she is. She is thoroughly immoral.' And the way Simon looked at things, no prophet, professing to be the mouthpiece of God, would allow an immoral woman to touch him. After all, God wouldn't.

In this last respect, of course, Simon was no doubt right. Holy Scripture unambiguously declares that nothing that defiles shall enter the presence of God. 'Dogs and sorcerers and the sexually immoral and murderers and idolaters, and everyone who loves and practises falsehood' are forever excluded from the eternal city (Rev 22:15). Heaven, at least, shall not be made into the foul place that earth has become.

But there was a curious blind spot in Simon's reasoning. He had invited Christ into his home without so much as a thought, apparently, as to whether—if Christ were a prophet—his own home was clean and holy enough to receive him. He had just assumed without thinking that it was. Not that he would have claimed that he was sinless; far from it. But then he was different from this woman: she was immoral, positively indecent. You couldn't exactly call any sin decent, but his own sins were the kind that decent and respectable people commit. They certainly weren't in his opinion anywhere near bad enough to make his home an unsuitable place for a prophet of the Almighty.

Degrees of sin

A voice was speaking across the table, and Simon came to with a start. 'Simon, I have something to say to you.' It was Christ. 'Say it, Teacher,' replied Simon. 'A certain money-lender had two debtors . . .' (Luke 7:40–41). With striking suitability, Christ chose the analogy that sin is like debt. If a man is in debt for £5,000,000 and cannot pay, he is bankrupt. If a man is in debt for only £5 and cannot pay, he is no less bankrupt. There may be no comparison in the amount of the debt, but the principle of bankruptcy is exactly the same. And if sin is like debt, then certainly the vices of the immoral have rendered them bankrupt before the bar of God's law; but then the sins of the respectable have rendered them no less bankrupt.

True, we tend to put different sins into different categories; though even in this it is conceivable, indeed highly probable, that God's categories may well be very different from ours. Nevertheless, we all know what we mean when we describe some sins as filthy, and the description serves a useful purpose of practical definition. But we should be careful not to let this practical distinction lead us to make the unconscious assumption that the 'non-filthy' sins (the category to which we prefer to think that the majority of our own sins belong) are in some sense clean. There are no clean sins. All sin defiles. There is admittedly a difference between a speck of soot and a ton of it, but the difference is solely in the quantity: in essential quality and character the speck is exactly the same as the ton. Sin of the sexual kind certainly unfits a person for the presence of God. But then there is no kind of sin that doesn't. In the truer sense of the word all sin is immoral.

'A certain money-lender had two debtors. One owed five hundred denarii, and the other fifty.' Christ was developing his parable; and if earlier Simon had been inwardly making his comparative estimates of sin, now evidently it was Christ's turn to do the comparing. In the amounts they owed, the debtors were very different, but they were exactly alike in this: neither of them could pay a thing, both were equally bankrupt. It really began to look as if Simon was in for a salutary lesson on not judging other people, and the parable was going to lead to the well-earned rebuke, 'Judge not, and you shall not be judged.' But at this point, Christ's parable took an unexpected turn, and went off in another direction completely.

'A certain money-lender had two debtors. One owed five hundred denarii, and the other fifty. When they could not pay, he cancelled the debt of both. Now which of them will love him more?' Simon was ready with the answer, for he was good at making comparisons. If, of course, you concentrate simply on the debts, there is no question that the bigger the debt is the more serious it is; and if, as is normal in the business world, the only way to get rid of the debt is to pay it back, the bigger the debt the greater the disadvantage the debtor is at, and the harder the effort they must exert to wipe the debt out.

But if you are going to introduce a creditor who is so extraordinarily merciful and generous that he is prepared to forgive the debt completely, just wipe it out without requiring any payment whatsoever, then it is quite obvious that the bigger the debt a person has been in, the more relief they will feel at it being cancelled, and the greater the gratitude they will show to their creditor. Simon said the obvious. Jesus asked, "'Now which of them will love him more?" Simon answered, "The one, I suppose, for whom he cancelled the larger debt'" (7:42–43). He had got the answer right.

Degrees of forgiveness

But the new element in the calculations was disconcerting. Free forgiveness! Full, frank, free forgiveness, the debt wiped out without a penny having to be paid; forgiveness that did not have to be deserved or merited, but was given to people who by definition had nothing with which to pay their debt. Yet there was no mistaking the implication of the analogy: if sin was like debt, then God was the forgiving creditor. It was shatteringly different from all Simon's preconceptions. He believed in forgiveness, of course. His psalms, his hymns, his Bible were full of the idea; and often in his prayers he besought God for it, while the priests in the temple pronounced it over the penitent as they brought their sacrifices.

And yet, whatever the theory and theology of it, in actual practice and experience the forgiveness he knew was nothing like this creditor's forgiveness. It forgave sundry items in his spiritual account from time to time, but the account remained, and in his heart of hearts he knew it was generally in the red. There was one consolation, he felt: the amount he owed, the gap between God's demands and his fulfilment of them, was not anywhere near so large as it was with people like this prostitute.

But there was a gap, and the forgiveness of a few items now and again did very little to close it. Daily, with rigorous effort and discipline, he did all he knew how to narrow the gap. He tried to reach a position where he might at least have grounds for hoping that God's mercy might move him to overlook what little amount of debt remained, and finally accept Simon into his heaven. But it was a position that after many years of sustained effort Simon had not yet reached; indeed, the gap seemed no narrower now than it ever had been. It began to look as if he might never reach it, but that was a prospect Simon never allowed himself to dwell on. Pride, perhaps fear, shut his mind to the stern logic of his situation: if the minimum requirement of God's law is constant perfection, no amount of perfection could ever wipe out the deficit of a single sin. Simon had nothing to pay his debt with. In this he was as bankrupt as the prostitute.

Degrees of love

But the voice across the table was still speaking: 'Simon, do you see this woman?' Of course he had seen her. But if Christ was going to say that she had had a sudden conversion, or had been 'saved,' then he wasn't prepared to believe it, and certainly not simply because Christ said it. But Christ wasn't saying it, at least not just yet. He was making some factual observations.

> I entered your house; you gave me no water for my feet, but she has wet my feet with her tears and wiped them with her hair. You gave me no kiss, but from the time I came in she has not ceased to kiss my feet. You did not anoint my head with oil, but she has anointed my feet with ointment. (7:44–46)

Comparisons again; but then it was Simon who had started it, and it was Simon who had so confidently asserted the obvious—when a man has been forgiven, he loves the person who forgave him, and the more he has been forgiven, the more he loves. And there was no disputing the fact that, although he had invited Christ to lunch, he had exhibited no particular love towards him. He had scarcely shown him the bare courtesies of the time, whereas 'this woman', as he called her, had shown the most extraordinary personal love and devotion to Christ. If love was evidence that forgiveness had been received, and no love was evidence that forgiveness had not been received. . .

With inexorable logic the voice was proceeding: 'On the grounds of this evidence I'm telling you that this woman's notorious sins, many as they were, have been forgiven. They must be, for look how much love she has shown me.' And then, turning to the woman, Christ spelt out in so many words what already the Holy Spirit's witness in her heart had made her feel: 'Your sins are forgiven' (7:48).

Not only Simon but all the lunch party saw the point. By an unfortunate inadequacy in the earlier English translations (happily made good by some modern versions like the Jerusalem Bible and the New International Version) whole generations of people have taken the Lord to mean that the woman received her forgiveness as a return for her love. In consequence they have tried by all manner of means to work up feelings of love towards God in the hope that, if only they could manage to love him enough, God would on that account be induced to forgive them. If nothing else, common experience ought to have made them realize how difficult, if not impossible, it is for a debtor to love his creditor while the debt is still outstanding and the creditor is still threatening proceedings. But apart from that, our Lord's parable had made it quite clear that the debtors did not get forgiveness because they loved their creditor; they only began to love him after and because they had been forgiven.

God's forgiveness

The guests at the lunch saw the point clearly and at once. What startled them was another implication in Christ's words. Like Simon, they were used to having the priests in the temple pronounce forgiveness over their heads when they brought and offered their sacrifices. But the priests pronounced forgiveness in the name of God, not in their own right, and at best left the verdict of the final judgment uncertain. Christ, they felt, was claiming to forgive sins in his own right and in the absolute and final sense. 'Who is this, who even forgives sins?' they said (7:49). They were, of course, perfectly correct in their feeling. Christ was acting here in his personal and absolute capacity as the final judge, as he himself elsewhere expressed it:

> The Father judges no one, but has given all judgement to the Son, that all may honour the Son, just as they honour the Father. Whoever does not honour the Son does not honour the Father who sent him. Truly, truly, I say to you, whoever hears my word and believes him who sent me has eternal life. He does not come into judgement, but has passed from death to life. (John 5:22–24)

Turning once more to the woman, he said: 'Your faith has saved you; go in peace' (Luke 7:50).

And so a fallen woman was saved, and made fit company for God's own Son. But when exactly did it happen? We cannot tell. Little is told us about her, except that by the time our Lord called Simon's attention to her, she had already been forgiven, so that Simon's objection to our Lord's reception of her was groundless. She had been immoral; she was so no longer. When the change took place we can only guess. But this we know, the change had not been produced by the kind of religion that Simon followed. His preaching against immorality was perfectly correct, biblical in fact, and necessary. But it had not produced a change in this woman. Once she had fallen, it simply drove her deeper into despair. How could the past be wiped out, even if she went straight for the rest of her life? And if the past could not be wiped out, how could she ever get back into decent society? And if she couldn't do that, what other way was left open to her, in the world in which she lived, of making a living except by continuing in her sin? And when Simon and his ilk, both by their preaching and their behaviour, made it obvious that they despised her, and regarded themselves as infinitely superior, her despair probably deepened into cynicism.

Some men in the town used her services. Did none of them go to Simon's synagogue? But one day she heard a different kind of preacher. He likewise preached against immorality, though with this difference—his teaching included the synagogue-goers too as morally bankrupt before God. But then he said that God was prepared to receive, welcome, and utterly forgive all who came in true repentance— that he, as God, had authority in the here and now to receive such just as they were, to forgive, cleanse, and sanctify them, and to admit them into the personal fellowship of God. On these terms he bade sinners to 'come to him' and in her simplicity she had taken him literally. She had come, braving the contempt, disgust and anger in almost every face at the table. But she had no sooner come than she knew his word was true. She was forgiven and received, and, oblivious of her surroundings, she had given vent to her relief and joy. Her gratitude was immediate evidence of her sense of forgiveness. But it was more; in the years that followed it became one of the motive powers of her transformed life. In the closing verses of his Gospel, Luke reminds us that there were many women like her, from all walks in life. Their gratitude did not merely issue in tears; it transformed them into practical, hard-working, and holy followers and servants of Christ.

Redeeming *a* Swindler

After this he went out and saw a tax collector named Levi, sitting at the tax booth. And he said to him, 'Follow me.' And leaving everything, he rose and followed him.

And Levi made him a great feast in his house, and there was a large company of tax collectors and others reclining at table with them. And the Pharisees and their scribes grumbled at his disciples, saying, 'Why do you eat and drink with tax collectors and sinners?'

And Jesus answered them, 'Those who are well have no need of a physician, but those who are sick. I have not come to call the righteous but sinners to repentance.'

Luke 5:27–32

The Son of Man has come eating and drinking, and you say, 'Look at him! A glutton and a drunkard, a friend of tax collectors and sinners!'

Luke 7:34

He also told this parable to some who trusted in themselves that they were righteous, and treated others with contempt: 'Two men went up into the temple to pray, one a Pharisee and the other a tax collector. The Pharisee, standing by himself, prayed thus: 'God, I thank you that I am not like other men, extortioners, unjust, adulterers, or even like this tax collector. I fast twice a week; I give tithes of all that I get.'

But the tax collector, standing far off, would not even lift up his eyes to heaven, but beat his breast, saying, 'God, be merciful to me, a sinner!'

I tell you, this man went down to his house justified, rather than the other. For everyone who exalts himself will be humbled, but the one who humbles himself will be exalted.'

Luke 18:9–14

He entered Jericho and was passing through. And there was a man named Zacchaeus. He was a chief tax collector and was rich. And he was seeking to see who Jesus was, but on account of the crowd he could not, because he was small of stature. So he ran on ahead and climbed up into a sycamore tree to see him, for he was about to pass that way.

And when Jesus came to the place, he looked up and said to him, 'Zacchaeus, hurry and come down, for I must stay at your house today.' So he hurried and came down and received him joyfully.

And when they saw it, they all grumbled, 'He has gone in to be the guest of a man who is a sinner.'

And Zacchaeus stood and said to the Lord, 'Behold, Lord, half of my goods I give to the poor. And if I have defrauded anyone of anything, I restore it fourfold.'

And Jesus said to him, 'Today salvation has come to this house, since he also is a son of Abraham. For the Son of Man came to seek and to save the lost.'

Luke 19:1–10

Income tax inspectors are scarcely popular figures. Generally they are the target of our wry humour, and sometimes, when we get our tax returns, the focus of some bitter thoughts. But, of course, in our saner moments we realize that they are honourable people doing a necessary, if unpopular, job.

The tax-collector of ancient Palestine, however, was an altogether different type of man. In the first place, he collected the taxes imposed by the hated Roman overlords. This made him in the eyes of Jews in general little short of a traitor, while to the extreme right wing—who resented the Roman occupation not only on nationalistic but also on religious grounds—he was an apostate as well as a traitor.

In the second place, the temptations inherent in the way Rome organized the tax collecting made him all too often a swindler. The Romans never actually collected the taxes themselves. They farmed them out to entrepreneurs. Whoever bought the right to collect them was free (as long as he paid into Rome the amount at which his area had been assessed) to make as much as he could for his own pocket. On top of that he could, if he wished, let out the rights at a profit to sub-contractors, who could in turn take a large extra slice of money from the populace for themselves. Many of the tax-collectors were utterly ruthless and became exceedingly wealthy.

Little wonder that the Jews regarded the whole class as despicably evil, and that the rabbis barred them from the synagogue. And when some of them professed repentance under John the Baptist's preaching, John warned them that they had not a hope of being regarded as sincere, unless they ceased immediately and permanently from their extortion (Luke 3:12–13).

When Christ, therefore, was frequently to be found in the company of tax-collectors, the Pharisees took great exception to it. They were not wildly enthusiastic about evangelical work of any kind, but if Christ must go missioning, there were plenty of respectable poor people that he could have tried to teach. Why must he always disregard the feelings of all decent people and openly associate with the despicable tax-collectors? This seemed to them to be nothing but condoning and conniving at open crime—a very cheap way to win support.

Then, if you please, Christ actually chose a tax-collector named Levi (also called Matthew) as one of his twelve special followers. Levi in turn held a great reception in his house to which he invited Christ and a number of other tax-collectors (5:27–32). To try and preach to tax-collectors was in the Pharisees' opinion futile; to eat with them socially was the extreme of questionable behaviour. 'Why do you eat and drink with tax collectors and sinners?' (5:30) they demanded of his disciples, in a mixture of embittered criticism and angry bewilderment.

Sinners need a Saviour

People still feel like this, and it is easy to call them all 'separatists' (what the name Pharisee means) and from the superior heights of a liberal outlook to pour down scorn on their narrow-mindedness. But we would do better to try and understand their feelings.

It is at least comprehensible, for instance, why those who have seen at first-hand the miseries inflicted on whole families by alcoholism object to a preacher going into a pub, even for the purpose of preaching the gospel. To them preaching in a pub would be almost like giving lectures on Jewish culture to the officers in a concentration camp. Or, to take another example, some congregations may well be wary of enthusiastic church workers bringing drug addicts into their services because parents are genuinely afraid that their own young people could become influenced to take drugs themselves. Moreover, there may be the fear that, if a church gets the reputation as a place where all sorts of questionable characters hang around, people in the neighbourhood could hesitate to come in, however much they might want spiritual help. Some sins are so blatantly anti-social that any religious community is obliged openly to excommunicate members who are guilty of those sins, or else completely forfeit credibility with the general public.

It was for this reason that the Pharisees banned tax-collectors from their synagogues, and why Christian churches are commanded by the Apostle Paul to excommunicate anyone who professes to be a Christian but is guilty of certain anti-social sins (1 Cor 5:1–13). It is not discipline of this kind that has impeded the progress of the gospel in the world at large, but the lack of it. All too often in the course of history the church has got itself into ill-repute by becoming identified with ruling classes who have oppressed the poor, and by tolerating members whose immoralities have been public knowledge.

New life

It is important, therefore, in this connection to notice what Christ did not do. Friend of tax-collectors and prostitutes though he was, he never tried to break the discipline of the synagogue by bringing groups of tax-collectors along to the synagogue services, any more than he tried to organize special services in the temple for prostitutes, or for the casts of disgustingly immoral shows as some modern clerics have done.

Levi had admittedly been a tax-collector before he became a disciple of Christ; but he did not continue to be afterwards. When Christ called him he was sitting at his tax-collector's post making his pile of extortionate profits; but, in answer to Christ's call, he left it to follow Christ and never went back. Christ did not take the view that, so long as some of the money went to support the Christian church, it did not matter how the money was made. And when Levi after his conversion held a reception so that many of his former colleagues could meet Christ, every tax-collector in the room knew—at the end of the reception if not at the beginning—exactly what both Levi and Christ were after. They were out to get the tax-collectors saved, to break their love of money and to finish their practice of extortion forever. But in order to save and rescue these men, Christ was prepared to meet them and eat and drink with them. The Pharisees objected to this too. Christ's answer to their objection was masterly and illuminating. 'Those who are well have no need of a physician, but those who are sick. I have not come to call the righteous but sinners to repentance' (Luke 5:31–32). By definition sin is nasty; some forms of it are highly infectious, and some sinners are mean and thoroughly rotten people. But it was sinners that Christ came to save.

What kind of doctor would refuse to go anywhere near the sick? If, for instance, someone develops meningitis, on the one hand it would be false kindness not to isolate them, and sheer criminality to allow just anybody to visit them. But on the other hand, if doctors and nurses stayed away the person would die. Not every Christian is called, or is spiritually mature enough, to be a missionary to every kind of sinner. But even people who have committed the most revolting forms of sin are human still, loved by God, and not to be given up as hopeless. Someone must go and find them, sit where they sit and tell them the gospel.

Indeed, some of them are more likely to respond to the gospel than the apparently decent and respectable churchgoer; and this is the point that our Lord makes in the next reference to tax-collectors in the Gospel of Luke:

> When all the people heard this [i.e., heard John the Baptist's preaching], and the tax collectors too, they declared God just, having been baptized with the baptism of John, but the Pharisees and the lawyers rejected the purpose of God for themselves, not having been baptized by him. (7:29–30)

Through John the Baptist God proclaimed that, in order to prepare themselves for the coming of Christ, men and women needed a radical repentance, a confession of their utter unworthiness, and this had to be symbolized by baptism in water. The tax-collectors found it comparatively easy to admit the justice of God's estimate: they were outright sinners and they knew it. But the Pharisees felt aggrieved and insulted. They were prepared to admit a small fault here and an odd sin or two there. But John's insistence that, in spite of all their religious discipline, they were still in themselves unworthy and in need of salvation struck them as an absurdly unjust exaggeration. They felt they were honest men, who had given themselves to fulfil the law of God to the utmost of their ability. Maybe they did come short a little, but not intentionally. They maintained that it was grotesque to describe them as moral failures and insist that they should be baptized on the same terms as tax-collectors.

They decided, therefore, that John had a demon and was emotionally unbalanced, and they refused his baptism. But what they refused, said Christ, was the counsel of God. By his standards of perfection they were failures. Moreover, by rejecting the counsel of God, they were adding positive rebellion to their failure and demonstrating that, apart from the experience of conversion, the religious heart is basically as much at enmity with God as the irreligious (see Rom 8:6–8). They stood in greater spiritual danger than the tax-collectors, because their religious disciplines camouflaged the fact that they were just as self-willed and independent of God as the person whose self-will expressed itself in crime.

A parable

This is the ever-present danger of the religiously inclined, and to combat it our Lord told the parable of the Pharisee and the Tax-collector (18:9–14). At first sight the parable is shocking. It seems to put a premium on evil living: the tax-collector 'went down to his house justified' (18:14). And it seems to despise and discourage moral effort: 'rather than the other'. But, of course, the parable was not intended to downgrade good works but to stop the abuse of them. It was spoken to 'some who trusted in themselves that they were righteous, and treated others with contempt' (18:9).

Two evils lurk in the attitude of such people. In the first place, they trust in themselves and in their righteous deeds, even coming before God and expecting him to accept them on the ground of their performance and attainment; and secondly, they despise others who have not performed as well as they have. Listen to the Pharisee at prayer: 'God, I thank you that I am not like other men, extortioners, unjust, adulterers, or even like this tax collector. I fast twice a week; I give tithes of all that I get' (18:11–12).

Now, in an athlete about to enter a one thousand metre race, such an attitude would be understandable; cut out the boasting and it would be quite acceptable. If the athlete has trained seriously and is at the very peak of his form, and his competitor has not trained but has smoked and got drunk, kept late nights and put on excessive weight, the athlete would be less than honest if he were not confident in his ability to beat his competitor and win the race. And when it comes to the work that true Christians are expected to do for God, Paul urges us that we ought to adopt this same attitude of an athlete in training. There are eternal prizes to be won by careful discipline and faithful toil, whereas carelessness may well lead to being disqualified from service (1 Cor 9:24–27).

Reward or gift?

But rewards for work well done, important and eternal as they are, are in an altogether different category from salvation and acceptance with God (see 1 Cor 3:10–15, noting especially v. 15). Our acceptance with God can never rest on our work; nor is salvation a competitive race in which the best performers get the first prizes. Our very best performance comes far short of God's standards of perfection, and God will never pretend that it is good enough to earn us his acceptance. On the other hand, what none of us can ever earn, he is prepared to give to all, if they will have it: divine acceptance and salvation as a free gift, given solely on the condition of repentance and faith. Listen to the tax-collector and Christ's comment on him:

> But the tax-collector, standing far off, would not even lift up his eyes to heaven, but beat his breast, saying, 'God, be merciful to me, a sinner!' I tell you, this man went down to his house justified, rather than the other.' (Luke 18:13–14)

It follows that if a comparatively good man has to be justified solely on the grounds of repentance and faith, altogether by God's grace, then in this respect he is in no way superior to the wickedest of men, and has no grounds for despising him or boasting in himself. He will cease to trust in himself that he is righteous, and will learn rather to adopt the attitude of Abraham who 'believed God, and it was counted to him as righteousness' (Rom 4:3–5).

At this point, however, most people meet a difficulty that makes it almost impossible for them to accept the doctrine that a person can be saved by faith without and apart from the works of the law, as Paul would put it (Rom 3:28). The difficulty is this: if a person's salvation did not depend on their keeping of God's law, and that person received salvation as a gift and knew themselves accepted by God, and they were sure that God would never reject them, then, so the argument goes, that person would take advantage of God's grace and live carelessly and sinfully. This was a difficulty that people who heard Paul preach used to throw up against him, and he answered it in his Letter to the Romans (6:1–4). But his travel companion, Luke, can help us over this difficulty, if we will consider one more story about a tax-collector and Christ.

Zacchaeus was not only a tax-collector; he was the chief of tax-collectors in the area. He was correspondingly ruthless and rich. The people had no way of avoiding his extortionate tax demands, but they let him know exactly what they thought of him. Everybody hated him; he was barred from the synagogue, and no ordinary person would have dreamed of having any social contact with him at all. When, therefore, Christ one day invited himself out to dinner at Zacchaeus' house, the crowd angrily murmured its disapproval. To accept such a man socially, they felt, would give him the impression that his unscrupulous conduct was acceptable, and encourage him to continue in it. But to the crowd's amazement, Christ had scarcely walked two steps along the road towards Zacchaeus' house when a miracle took place. Zacchaeus suddenly stopped in his tracks and said, 'Behold, Lord, half of my goods I give to the poor. And if I have defrauded anyone of anything, I restore it fourfold' (Luke 19:8). And so, what years of being preached at and being socially ostracized had failed to effect in the man, Christ's acceptance of him produced in a few minutes. How was it done?

Good works

We cannot, of course, know everything that went on in the man's heart, but Luke has given us some very obvious pointers. First of all, though Christ had accepted him as he was, he did not accept him without evidence of repentance. When Christ met him, Zacchaeus was, of all the odd places, up a tree. Christ could read his heart and knew well why he was in that strange position: he wanted to see Jesus. All his money-making, all his sense of power over people, had failed to satisfy him. He was now seeking 'to see who Jesus was' (19:3). He doubtless had heard of Christ's ethical teaching, and knew in his heart of hearts that it was right. But now he wanted to see what kind of man Jesus was.

Zacchaeus was a little man himself; that was why he was up the tree, so that he could see over the heads of the crowd. But he was a little man in more senses than one, or else he would never have taken such delight in exacting extortionate taxes out of poor people who had difficulty in making ends meet. Perhaps, indeed, being very short, he may early in life have developed a deep-seated inferiority complex and a feeling of rejection, which was forever driving him on to try and prove his 'superiority'. He turned to making money, perhaps with the subconscious idea that by becoming exceedingly wealthy he would make people respect him. In actual fact it only made them despise him and avoid his company. That in turn only increased his sense of rejection, and made him determine all the more to get his own back, demonstrating his superiority by hurting people and exacting ever more taxes from them, while filling his own house with extravagantly rich furniture, designed to impress everybody with his wealth and provoke their envy.

It was an endless and vicious spiral. How could it be broken? Not by more ethical teaching—Zacchaeus already knew his conduct was wrong; but in a very real sense he could not help himself. He was driven to it by urges that he did not understand and could not control. And social ostracism only made those urges stronger. Reading in his desire to see Jesus the faint beginnings of repentance—the bleating of a sheep that has got itself caught in a thicket and doesn't know how to get out—Christ cut through all the entanglements by accepting the man as he was. And he publicly demonstrated that acceptance by calling him down from the tree and announcing that he was coming to stay in his home.

At last, by the unmerited grace of God Zacchaeus had found what years of his own misguided toil had never been able to achieve—the sense of acceptance not only with men but at the highest level with the Creator himself. What was the effect on Zacchaeus? More extortion and endless taking advantage of the grace of God? No. He quit his extortion immediately and announced a magnificent programme of philanthropy—not in order to try and persuade Christ to accept him but simply because Christ had accepted him. 'Today salvation has come to this house,' commented Christ, 'since he also is a son of Abraham' (19:9).

To understand the point of Christ's comment one should perhaps read at length the writings of both Paul and James, which point out how Abraham's justification by faith led to such works as demonstrated that his faith was genuine. But that would be a long study. Let us content ourselves with the example of one of Abraham's greatest admirers, Paul himself. Before he was converted, while he still thought that salvation depended on his own merit and the keeping of God's law, Paul was one of the biggest hatred-filled, pride-filled, bigots of all time. When he discovered that salvation did not depend on his merits but was solely by the grace of God, he quit persecution, overcame his narrow Jewish exclusivism and embraced the whole Gentile world in his affections. At the cost of comfort, career, social standing, and eventually life itself, he devoted himself to serving his fellow men with a life and message of love that have altered the course of European, and indeed of world, history ever since.

STORY THREE

Avenging *the* Widow

And there was a prophetess, Anna, the daughter of Phanuel, of the tribe of Asher. She was advanced in years, having lived with her husband seven years from when she was a virgin, and then as a widow until she was eighty-four. She did not depart from the temple, worshipping with fasting and prayer night and day. And coming up at that very hour she began to give thanks to God and to speak of him to all who were waiting for the redemption of Jerusalem.

Luke 2:36–38

But in truth, I tell you, there were many widows in Israel in the days of Elijah, when the heavens were shut up three years and six months, and a great famine came over all the land, and Elijah was sent to none of them but only to Zarephath, in the land of Sidon, to a woman who was a widow.

Luke 4:25–26

Soon afterwards he went to a town called Nain, and his disciples and a great crowd went with him. As he drew near to the gate of the town, behold, a man who had died was being carried out, the only son of his mother, and she was a widow, and a considerable crowd from the town was with her. And when the Lord saw her, he had compassion on her and said to her, 'Do not weep.'

Then he came up and touched the bier, and the bearers stood still. And he said, 'Young man, I say to you, arise.' And the dead man sat up and began to speak, and Jesus gave him to his mother.

Fear seized them all, and they glorified God, saying, 'A great prophet has arisen among us!' and 'God has visited his people!' And this report about him spread through the whole of Judea and all the surrounding country.

Luke 7:11–17

And he told them a parable to the effect that they ought always to pray and not lose heart. He said, 'In a certain city there was a judge who neither feared God nor respected man. And there was a widow in that city who kept coming to him and saying, 'Give me justice against my adversary.'

For a while he refused, but afterwards he said to himself, 'Though I neither fear God nor respect man, yet because this widow keeps bothering me, I will give her justice, so that she will not beat me down by her continual coming.''

And the Lord said, 'Hear what the unrighteous judge says. And will not God give justice to his elect, who cry to him day and night? Will he delay long over them? I tell you, he will give justice to them speedily. Nevertheless, when the Son of Man comes, will he find faith on earth?'

Luke 18:1–8

And in the hearing of all the people he said to his disciples, 'Beware of the scribes, who like to walk around in long robes, and love greetings in the market-places and the best seats in the synagogues and the places of honour at feasts, who devour widows' houses and for a pretence make long prayers. They will receive the greater condemnation.'

Jesus looked up and saw the rich putting their gifts into the offering box, and he saw a poor widow put in two small copper coins. And he said, 'Truly, I tell you, this poor widow has put in more than all of them. For they all contributed out of their abundance, but she out of her poverty put in all she had to live on.'

Luke 20:45–21:4

Luke shows a remarkable concern for widows. In his pages we meet more widows than in any other book of the New Testament, or of the Old for that matter. Anna the prophetess, the woman who fed Elijah at Zarephath, the mother from the village of Nain who was burying her only son, the woman who pleaded for redress in the parable of the Unjust Judge—all these were widows, and Luke is the only evangelist to mention them. At the same time, of course, he mentions what the other evangelists also record—our Lord's denunciation of the scribes for extorting money from widows under religious pretence, and his commendation of the widow who voluntarily cast into the temple treasury the two small coins, which were her whole means of life.

The general impression that Luke's description of these widows conveys is not so much their grief at the loss of their husbands—on that score one might equally pity a husband who had lost his wife, or a father who had lost his child—but rather the feature of widowhood that most struck the ancient world: the widow's helplessness and defencelessness after her husband had gone. In ancient times there was no widow's pension, no social security benefits. What was worse, there was no career open to a widow, or, at least, no career that was morally decent. Unless she had adequate resources, therefore, it was a continual problem for her simply to get enough to live on. Her plight was naturally much relieved if she had a grown son or other adult male relatives, for they would assume responsibility for her. But if she was 'truly a widow', as the New Testament phrases it (1 Tim 5:5)—that is, if she had no male relatives capable of supporting her—her life was very hard.

Even suppose she had some private income, property, or business, she was often a prey to tricksters and unscrupulous businessmen, who would rob and cheat her. She could, of course, appeal to the local judge to protect and avenge her: but all too often he either could not be bothered to help her, or he was in the pay of the businessmen and not prepared to.

Religion would offer the widow its comforts, and these certainly were not to be despised. The pious and God-fearing, particularly among the Israelites, counted relief of the widow one of their foremost religious duties. On the other hand, officialdom in the shape of the religious scribes would often exact temple taxes and other religious dues even from widows who could by no means afford them.

All in all, then, the plight of widows was hard and unenviable. It is not surprising, therefore, that many a widow was driven by her need and defencelessness to a greater dependence on God, and a more sincere use of prayer than most of us are given to. Indeed, both among Jews and Christians, some widows devoted themselves entirely to a life of prayer, and were apparently in that case maintained by the community. Anna, the prophetess, Luke tells us, 'did not depart from the temple, worshipping with fasting and prayer night and day' (Luke 2:37). While Paul, in giving directions for the financial support of widows (1 Tim 5:3–10), describes 'truly a widow' as one who 'has set her hope on God and continues in supplications and prayers night and day'.

A social conscience

From these last observations it is clear that Luke's marked concern for widows does not mean that he alone of the early Christians had a social conscience. He himself records that one of the very first social duties undertaken by the infant church at Jerusalem was the daily care and maintenance of the widows (Acts 6:1–6). Moreover, the Christians had inherited this social conscience from Judaism and its Old Testament. The ancient code of Deuteronomy shows a remarkably humane concern for the poor and weak in general and for widows in particular. The patriarch, Job, in protesting the integrity of his way of life, lists high among his virtues that no widow had ever looked to him for help and been disappointed (Job 31:16). And when the Old Testament prophets denounce the nation for its wickedness, as alas they often have to, and list examples of their more outrageous sins, neglect and oppression of the widow generally stand high in the list (see, for example, Isa 1:23).

While concern for the widow was enjoined on all, it was regarded by the Old Testament as the special concern of the rulers and judges. The verse in Isaiah is in fact a denunciation of the government for its political and social sins: 'Your princes are rebels and companions of thieves. Everyone loves a bribe and runs after gifts. They do not bring justice to the fatherless, and the widow's cause does not come to them.'

And the extreme grievousness of their sin was heightened by the fact that in Israel the government and the judiciary were regarded as the representatives of God. Their dispensing of justice was supposed to be a reflection of the character of God, and an extension of his government. When Deuteronomy, their law code, wants to give some examples of the incomparability of God and the incorruptibility of his government, it cites as its very first example God's concern for the widow: 'For the LORD your God is God of gods and Lord of lords, the great, the mighty and the awesome God, who is not partial and takes no bribe. He executes justice for the fatherless and the widow . . .' (Deut 10:17–18).

Consequently, when the princes and judges in Israel neglected to look after the widows and even took bribes from the unscrupulous in order to deny widows justice in their courts, their behaviour constituted not only a social scandal but a blasphemous misrepresentation of the Almighty.

We should pause here to make sure that we understand clearly what the Old Testament means when it talks of God as 'executing justice for the widow'. The wording of some Bible translations might perhaps conjure up a picture of a court in which the widow appears as defendant to answer for her misdeeds. But that would be the very opposite of what the phrase means. It implies rather a court where the widow can appear as plaintiff to appeal for justice against those who have been cheating or oppressing her. The thought of appearing before this bar of divine justice fills her, therefore, not with gloom and fear, but with hope and joy. To her the fact of coming judgment is not a threat, but a veritable gospel. Let God only be willing to rouse himself and act on her behalf, then his verdict and his enforcement of it will bring the end of all her misery, and the restoration of the rights and possessions which neighbours, dealers, unscrupulous businessmen, and perhaps even the government have filched from her.

It is not a question of getting revenge on her enemies, or necessarily wishing to see them punished; but simply a matter of getting back her property or rights, or having a stop put to the oppression and suffering that she has had to endure. Generations of Jewish widows, then, were encouraged to comfort themselves with the belief that God was a God who executed justice for the widow. And not only widows. All who cared for justice and fair play, and saw widows and others being cheated or oppressed by the strong and unscrupulous, and yet had no power to intervene and put a stop to it, consoled themselves with the thought that one day God would intervene.

Judgment when?

But if God is a God who executes justice for the widow and the oppressed, when and how does he do it? Obviously not every day of the week. Even the prophets who most emphasize the fact that God cares for widows by denunciating their oppressors give evidence that such oppressors were all too common in their day, and that they succeeded in carrying on their nefarious business without constant interventions from the Almighty.

To the prophets, God's interventions were to be seen in two kinds of situation. The one kind were major catastrophes in the nation's life. Ezekiel, for instance, asserts that the nation's defeat, humiliation and exile at the hands of the Babylonians were God's judgment on the nation, and particularly upon its political and religious leaders for their oppression of the poor and the widows (Ezek 22:23–31). Zechariah not only agrees but warns his people that if they fail to learn their lesson from this exile, God will bring yet worse defeat and exile upon them.

The other kind of situation was the coming of the Messiah. In Malachi's day, for instance, the mood of the nation was to doubt whether God ever did or ever would intervene: 'Where is the God of justice?' (Mal 2:17) they cynically demanded. Malachi's answer was first his famous prophecy of the coming of Messiah's forerunner: 'Behold, I send my messenger, and he will prepare the way before me' (3:1). Then he gave a further prophecy of the coming of Messiah himself to purge the nation:

> Then I will draw near to you for judgement. I will be a swift witness against the sorcerers, against the adulterers, against those who swear falsely, against those who oppress the hired worker in his wages, the widow and the fatherless, against those who thrust aside the sojourner, and do not fear me, says the LORD of hosts. (3:5)

Therefore, in the centuries that followed Malachi's prophecy, the weak and the widows pinned their faith to the coming of the Messiah. And not only widows: the nation as a whole—when it lost its political independence and was oppressed by the great Gentile powers, and sometimes persecuted for its religious faith—came to feel very much like a widow, and looked and prayed for the coming of the Messiah to deliver it from its oppressors.

It was not without significance then that, when Mary and Joseph took our Lord into the temple as a babe, the prophetess Anna, who spoke to the bystanders about him, was herself a widow. In her own life she had known the desolation of widowhood, and it had turned her into a woman who waited on God continually. But as she prayed, her thoughts were not merely on her own personal needs: she was 'waiting for the redemption of Jerusalem' (Luke 2:38), for the coming of Messiah to deliver her nation from subservience to the oppressors. Recognizing Jesus as the Messiah, she spoke of him to all who, like her, were looking for that redemption.

Some thirty years later when John the Baptist appeared, announced himself as the forerunner prophesied by Malachi, and pointed to Jesus as the Messiah come to judge his people, hopes ran high among the faithful. Now at long last the widow and all the oppressed would be avenged. But Christ seemingly dashed their hopes. They expected that the kingdom of God was immediately to appear, and to correct their mistaken supposition he told a parable. 'A nobleman went into a far country to receive for himself a kingdom and then return' (see Luke 19:11–27). The meaning was clear: he must first go away, and not until he came again would he begin the work of judgment and avenge the oppressed.

He told also the parable of the Widow and the Unjust Judge (18:1–8), which encouraged his followers with the assurance that God would eventually avenge his elect who cry unto him day and night. However, it also warned them that God would not do it at once, but would be long-suffering over them; so much so that when the Son of Man eventually returned, people would have almost given up faith that there was going to be any judgment at all.

And no wonder, for here we touch on a problem that is faith's most severe test. If there is a God who cares for justice, why does he allow evil to go unchecked? If Jesus Christ is really his Son, why did he not fulfil the promise of the prophets and avenge the oppressed when he was here on earth? The New Testament promises that he will come again and judge the world. But nearly two thousand years have passed and the promise has not been fulfilled. In the meanwhile, to go no further than the Jewish nation, in the desolation of her widowhood she has suffered the most ghastly persecutions and oppressions, often at the hands of those who have professed to be the followers of Christ. How can we believe the promise?

A moral sense

Here are problems enough: let us attempt some answers. First, if there is a God who cares for justice why does he not intervene when a widow is cheated and remove the cheater; or, better still, remove or prevent the cheater before he can do his cheating? That way there would be no sinners. Quite so, but there would be no saints either. Indeed, there would no longer be human beings. The difference between a human being and a mere animal is that the human does not work simply by instinct: he or she has moral sense.

To develop a true personal morality a person must further be given responsibilities and a free choice in the exercise of those responsibilities. For instance, if I know that there is a thousand pounds in the boss's cash box on the table, and that if I stole the box I could easily get away with it, I have a real choice in front of me whether to steal it or not, and therefore a moral decision to make. But if I happen to know that the box is wired up to a lethal dose of electric current, my decision not to steal it is no longer a moral decision. I have no choice in the matter. I may be the biggest rogue in the world, but unless I want to commit suicide, I cannot even touch the box.

Extend that to every possible sin and to every person in the world. If we knew that the moment we did a wrong deed or adopted a wrong attitude, we should immediately be cut off by some lightning stroke of God's judgment, we might manage to abstain from sinning. But our abstinence would not indicate that we were genuinely moral people. We should in fact be nothing more than Pavlovian-conditioned dogs.

Again, if we are to develop moral stature, we must be given responsibilities and allowed to discharge them. God loves children, but he does not personally attend to the upbringing and education of each child. He has given that responsibility to parents and teachers. But if the first time a parent or teacher failed in their care for a child, or indeed committed any sin whatever, they were cut off by God's judgment, how many parents or teachers would last out the first week of their apprenticeship? The fact is there would very soon be no parents or teachers left. And the same goes for judges and politicians, businessmen, and indeed for us all.

This being so, we need to change our point of view for a moment. So far we have been talking about widows and their oppressors, and naturally we tend to identify ourselves with the widows: the people who are sinned against rather than the sinning. And it may be true that in life we have been sinned against most grievously. As long as this is our only perspective, we shall find it very difficult to understand why God does not judge sinners the moment they sin. But when we come to see that we too have sinned against others, and to that extent we must be identified with the oppressors rather than the oppressed, we shall then not be so concerned to ask why God does not immediately judge the oppressors, but rather if there is any deliverance for them. Can they be rescued from their cruelty, evil urges and selfishness that twist them and drive them to sin?

Deliverance for oppressors

The answer to the question is, 'Yes', and it was beautifully put by Christ in the sermon he preached in the synagogue in his hometown of Nazareth (Luke 4:16–30). There is a passage in the prophet Isaiah which runs as follows:

> The Spirit of the Lord GOD is upon me,
>> because the LORD has anointed me
> to bring good news to the poor;
>> he has sent me to bind up the broken-hearted,
> to proclaim liberty to the captives,
>> and the opening of the prison to those who are bound;
> to proclaim the year of the LORD's favour,
>> and the day of vengeance of our God. (Isa 61:1–2)

This was of course a prophecy of what Messiah would do when he came; and at first sight it looked as if its glorious programme of deliverance for the oppressed would be accomplished by Messiah putting God's judgment on the oppressors into action.

Christ read this passage in the synagogue. But when he got as far as the phrase 'the year of the Lord's favour' (Luke 4:19), he broke off, and without reading the next phrase, 'the day of vengeance of our God' (Isa 61:2), he shut the book and said, 'Today this Scripture has been fulfilled in your hearing' (Luke 4:21).

It was a dramatic gesture. He was indisputably claiming to be the Messiah. He was claiming to have come in order to relieve the oppressed and liberate the prisoners. But equally emphatically he was declaring that at this stage he was not going to institute God's judgment on the oppressors. It was not that he did not believe in the execution of judgment. On other occasions he spoke with great solemnity of the universal judgment that will accompany his second coming (see for instance Luke 17:22–37; 21:5–36).

But at Christ's first coming he was as much concerned to liberate the oppressors as he was to liberate the oppressed. Men like the tax-collector doubtless oppressed and swindled the widows in their district. But they did so because they themselves were slave-driven by lusts and complexes that they could not control. Saul of Tarsus hounded people into literal prisons, because he himself was imprisoned in the infinitely worse prison of religious bigotry. To have instituted the day of God's vengeance would certainly have relieved one class of prisoner, but it would have put the other class beyond the hope of deliverance forever.

Moreover, when compassion for the widow has made all legitimate allowances, it must be admitted that the widows themselves were not sinless. Their sins, though less lurid, imprisoned them as much as tax-collectors' sins imprisoned them. It was best even for the widows that Christ did not at once institute the day of judgment.

This delay in the coming of the day of judgment, however, must sorely try the faith of those who are then obliged to endure outrage and injustice. Indeed, the bitterest element in their suffering could well be the doubt that might arise, whether there was after all a God who cared for justice; or was their suffering simply the meaningless product of a materialistic and fundamentally amoral universe? Christ indicated as much in his parable of the Widow and the Unjust Judge. But this testing of faith is not a disaster. It is not even an awkward but unavoidable consequence of God's determination to save as many sinners as possible. If we are to believe Peter (1 Pet 1:6–9), it is a necessary process in the strengthening of that faith to the point where it will enable the believer to enjoy to the maximum the inheritance that lies before them in the age to come.

Faith necessary

There remains, however, the biggest question of all. The reasons we have given to explain why God does not immediately intervene to avenge the widow and to put down oppression may in themselves be logical and convincing, but how can we be sure they are true and not merely our attempts to rationalize our wishful thinking? Luke tells us that this was the question uppermost in the minds of the people of Nazareth as they listened to Christ in the synagogue. They had heard of the physical miracles that he had done in Capernaum, but they felt they wanted more evidence before they could be expected to believe him.

But he declined to do any miracles in their presence. Instead he quoted an incident from the Old Testament: 'But in truth, I tell you, there were many widows in Israel in the days of Elijah, when the heavens were shut up three years and six months, and a great famine came over all the land, and Elijah was sent to none of them but only to Zarephath, in the land of Sidon, to a woman who was a widow' (Luke 4:25–26).

This enraged them. First, because it touched their pride in reminding them that, though they were nationally the descendants of faithful Abraham, they were at times less willing to believe their prophets than the Gentiles were. And second, it enraged them because they felt that their request for more evidence in the shape of physical miracles before they would believe was quite reasonable, and that in refusing it Christ was evading the issue.

He wasn't, of course. Physical miracles certainly provided ample initial evidence that he was someone special, but there comes a point when merely to repeat that kind of evidence adds nothing to the final proof. What is needed is a different kind of evidence. As Messiah, he claimed to be able to free people from their slavery to evil habits, complexes and sin. His physical miracles gave evidence that his claims were to be taken seriously, but the final proof for any individual that Christ could effect such deliverance would only come as they personally committed themselves to him and allowed Christ to do his work of deliverance within them. And here, in the nature of things, the act of faith in committing oneself to Christ would have to come before having the final proof that Christ's claim was true. But the people at Nazareth were not prepared to take that step of faith. Why not?

The story of the Sidonian widow can throw light on the problem. When she met Elijah, she had only enough food left for one more meal and then she was going to lie down and die. Elijah told her that if she would first make him a meal from that food, God would then miraculously maintain her food supply until the end of the famine. It was a tremendous test. If she took Elijah at his word and he then turned out to be a fraud, she had lost her last bite of food and imminent death would stare her in the face. What made her stake all she had on Elijah's word?

The fact is that it was easier for her than might appear at first sight. She was a widow, utterly without resources. Even if she refused to trust Elijah and kept her food for herself, it was such a minute quantity that death was still imminent. On the other hand, if she gave the food to Elijah and he turned out to be a fraud, she had lost very little. Death would come a few hours sooner, that was all. But if she dared commit herself to Elijah and he turned out to be true, she was saved. She had virtually nothing to lose but everything to gain.

If, however, she had not been a widow—if she had had slightly more food, say a basketful instead of a handful, she might well have been tempted to trust her own resources in the hope that somehow they would see her through the famine. And then, because she was depending on her own meagre resources, she may well have been afraid to take the step of faith and give Elijah anything.

The problem of self

So it was with the people of Nazareth. Christ's physical miracles had furnished evidence that he was at least a prophet: this much they knew and did not deny. But when he claimed that he had come as Messiah to deliver people from their sinful attitudes and habits, they would not have any evidence in their own lives personally that he could indeed do this unless they were prepared to commit themselves to him and allow him to do his work within them.

They were not prepared to take this step of faith. They saw no immediate and compelling need for it. They were moral, upright and spiritually resourceful people. What was wrong with the world was other people. If Christ could miraculously launch a few thunderbolts and eliminate all immoral tax-collectors; if by miraculous power he could drive out the hated Romans and give them their political freedom; if he would constantly repeat his miracles of multiplying the loaves and fishes—then of course they would hail him as their political Messiah.

But to insist that their sinful attitudes and deeds were a contributory factor to the world's misery was going too far. They weren't that bad. They were not resourceless spiritual widows; they could manage to put their own lives right. Perhaps so far they had not been too successful. But then you can't be always worrying whether the attitudes you adopt and the things you do to other people are selfish and sinful. It is a hard world, and you have to look after number one. And anyway, who was he to suggest that they needed to be saved?

They flew into a temper, rose up, bustled him out of their synagogue, and tried to throw him down a nearby cliff. The explosive violence of their reaction suggests that Christ had put his finger on a hidden guilt complex. Perhaps the anger with which they normally denounced Romans, tax-collectors, swindlers and oppressors had after all been fed in part by the smouldering fires of their own uneasy, guilty conscience. Shame and fear had done their best to suppress it. They had tried to compensate for their uneasiness by an exaggerated devotion to external religious rites, like the ceremonial washing of hands and the observance of holy days. But now Christ's suggestion that, orthodox as they were, they needed to be saved had penetrated to their conscience and made it erupt. It is astonishing how violently some people react to the suggestion that they need to be saved, but can we be sure that in telling the story Luke has not got his eye on us?

STORY FOUR

Converting
a
Criminal

One of the criminals who were hanged railed at him, saying, 'Are you not the Christ? Save yourself and us!'

But the other rebuked him, saying, 'Do you not fear God, since you are under the same sentence of condemnation? And we indeed justly, for we are receiving the due reward of our deeds; but this man has done nothing wrong.'

And he said, 'Jesus, remember me when you come into your kingdom.'

And he said to him, 'Truly, I say to you, today you will be with me in Paradise.'

Luke 23:39–43

The story of the so-called dying thief is very well known. And it deserves to be. It illustrates as few other stories do the almost incredible extent of the forgiveness of God. After a life of lurid crime, a professional criminal in the eleventh hour, indeed in the fifty-ninth minute of the eleventh hour, repents and trusts Christ; and Christ forgives him immediately and absolutely.

This demonstrates too the astoundingly great effect of God's salvation. No sooner had the criminal repented and trusted Christ than Christ not only forgave him but assured him that on that very same day he would be with Christ in paradise. There was to be no long period of waiting until his character was purified. Clearly there was going to be no opportunity on earth for the ordinary disciplines of life to refine him: that day was his last. Nightfall would find him dead and buried. But just as clearly the Saviour's words indicated that there was to be no long period after death during which he would have to be purified until he eventually became fit to be introduced into the immediate presence of the Saviour. 'Today you will be with me in Paradise,' said Christ (23:43).

Today: no delay. With me: no distance. In paradise: no more pain or suffering. The story is not only well known it is well loved, and no wonder.

Repentance

The purpose of our study, however, is first to observe how genuine the criminal's repentance and conversion were, and then to trace the steps by which he came to such repentance and faith. First, notice his unqualified confession: 'We are receiving the due reward of our deeds' (23:41). Unlike his fellow criminal, he no longer screams or wheedles to be let off the temporal punishment for his crimes. Nor does he attempt to plead excuses or provoke sympathy. Unreservedly he admits his guilt and accepts that he is justly punished.

Second, notice the terms of his surrender: 'Jesus, remember me when you come into your kingdom' (23:42). It is interesting that he makes no explicit request for forgiveness, though of course forgiveness is implied in his request. His explicit plea is for something more positive. The prostitute Rahab implored the Israelite spies that, when they returned with the armies of Israel to take the land, they would spare her and her family, and allow them to become members of the kingdom of Israel (Josh 2). So this criminal was asking Christ that, when Christ came again in power and glory to take up his universal dominion, Christ would spare him and accept him as a member of his kingdom. For him to ask this was highly significant.

We cannot be sure exactly what kind of criminal the man was. Certainly he was no petty house thief, for Matthew describes him by a word that normally in Greek means a robber, brigand or bandit. The uncertainty arises because the historian Josephus uses the term of political activists who were prepared to use the murderous methods of the bandit to further their political cause. But whatever type of murderer our criminal was, he had clearly lived his life in defiance of government. An outlaw himself, he had no respect even for the mere basic rules of fair play and humanity.

Now, however, he repents. He gives up his anarchy and asks to be admitted into a kingdom as an obedient subject of its king. From now on he will count it a favour to be governed and to submit to authority. He will submit of his own free will, gladly and ungrudgingly. This is repentance. It is required of us all and not merely of criminals. While we may have been loyal, law-abiding citizens in our relations with our country, it has been otherwise in our relations with God. The Bible does not charge us all alike with grievous anti-social crime. But it does charge us all alike with having 'gone astray; we have turned—every one—to his own way', and therefore it calls on us to repent in this fashion: 'Let the wicked forsake his way, and the unrighteous man his thoughts; let him return to the LORD, that he may have compassion on him' (see Isa 53:6 and 55:7).

Faith

Thirdly, we may notice that this repentance had been induced in him when he came to believe in the objective fact of the second coming of Christ: 'remember me when you come into your kingdom' (Luke 23:42); that is, when you come again in your kingly power to reign. But at this moment Christ was about to die. Evidently, then, the man had come to believe that, in spite of dying on a cross, Christ would one day come again to reign. A similar faith is required in us too if we would be saved. Hear Paul lay down the conditions of salvation: 'If you confess with your mouth that Jesus is Lord and believe in your heart that God raised him from the dead, you will be saved' (Rom 10:9).

But what had induced in this hardened criminal such a certain faith in the world to come? To this we may not be able to give the full answer, but we can at least listen to him rebuking his fellow criminal and observe how his mind ran. The other criminal openly reviled Jesus: 'Are you not the Christ? Save yourself and us!' (Luke 23:39). There was not the slightest grain of faith in his words; nothing but the bitterest mockery.

To him religion and all its claims were nothing but the tool of the ruling classes, who used it to oppress the poor and to hunt and persecute people like himself. Even in the face of imminent death he cursed religion in total unbelief of all it stood for.

But presently the other criminal began to rebuke him, 'Do you not fear God?' (23:40). It was one thing to curse religion as interpreted by faulty and perhaps even corrupt religious leaders. But God was different. Didn't he even fear him? But then why should he fear him? How could he even be sure that God existed? Or, if he existed, that death did not automatically mean annihilation for mankind, and therefore make God irrelevant?

But the second criminal had his reasons, for in spite of his excruciating pain he had been watching and thinking. 'Do you not fear God, since you are under the same sentence of condemnation?' (23:40). The same condemnation as who? He could not have been referring to himself. For one criminal to find himself condemned along with another criminal was hardly remarkable. He must have meant then, 'You are in the same condemnation as Christ.' But how could it be significant that he found himself condemned along with Christ?

Well, to start with, the religious leaders had hated and condemned Christ too. Both criminals hated them because they represented the Establishment which had persecuted and hounded them. In fact, at this moment these same religious leaders were strutting backwards and forwards in front of the three crosses, openly deriding and taunting Christ. It was clear enough that Christ was not altogether on the side of the Establishment. Indeed, at this moment he had more in common with the two criminals than with them.

But that was not all. 'You got the same sentence as he did, but in our case we deserved it: we are paying for what we did. But this man has done nothing wrong' (JB). Yes, Jesus was patently innocent, and compared with him they had to admit that they deserved what they were getting. They might curse the authorities for having been involved in shady deals themselves. But they knew in their heart of hearts that what the authorities were doing to them, they themselves had often done to other people. They could not expect anything else than the most violent punishment. But this Jesus was innocent. At the very least he deserved their sympathy, not their cursing.

Conversion

But there was still more to it. As the two criminals and Jesus had been led under guard to the place of crucifixion, some women from Jerusalem had followed Jesus, weeping and bewailing him. And Jesus had turned and told them not to weep for him but rather for themselves. The day of judgment was coming and their nation would yet have to face God over the crime that they were now perpetrating. What then about this day of judgment? Was it a reality, or just one more bogey invented by the religious Establishment to frighten and cow the likes of him and his fellow criminal? Well, this Jesus did not agree with the Establishment, that was obvious; but he did believe in the coming judgment.

And then there was another thing. The fiendish authorities beneath the cross not only sentenced their victims to death, but took delight in taunting them in their tortured agonies. Their preaching of judgment was perhaps little more than an expression of their own sadism. But this Jesus, though he believed in coming judgment, had actually prayed God's forgiveness for the soldiers during the very moments when they were driving the nails through his hands. Here was not only innocence but unearthly goodness. And yet here he was, being brutally murdered by these rotten hypocrites at the foot of the cross.

In a few hours death would end their pain. But would it end everything? Would death simply annihilate the guilty with the innocent and so forever perpetuate the injustices of their life? Was there in the end no difference between wrong and right? No! It could not be. Criminal though he was, even he cared about right and wrong and fair play. Strangely enough, thinking about Christ, he found he cared just now more than ever he'd done, even though caring for Christ's innocent suffering made him by comparison realize his own guilt all the more vividly.

Conscience can seem a strange thing. He certainly hadn't invented it. When he had been out on a 'job', it had often proved a most unwelcome intruder, and he had had to clobber it hard and suppress it. Right now, if he could manage to suppress it, he could die in peace. But he didn't want to suppress it or deny it. If conscience was a delusion, then his enemies, foul hypocrites that they were, would get off unpunished. But worse. This beautiful character, Jesus, and all that was fair and dear in life would perish indiscriminately with the foul and the filthy.

No! There was a God, and conscience was his voice. Then if there was a God who cared for the difference between right and wrong, who cared for justice and fair play, there certainly would be a resurrection and a judgment after death in which the injustices of this world would be put right. And if there was a coming judgment, they too had to face it. This was no time to be cursing Christ or even the Establishment. They had enough to answer for themselves. It was time they tried to get ready to meet God. Rounding on his fellow criminal who was still cursing and reviling Christ, he shouted him down. 'Don't you even fear God? Can't you see that you have been condemned along with him; but we have got a just sentence, we deserve everything we've got, whereas he has never done anything wrong.'

But at once his thoughts were back with himself. How was he to get right with God? His past held no merit. To promise reform in the future was useless: he had but a few hours left, spiked hand and foot to a cross. Soon the pain that was tearing through every fibre of his body and searing his brain would make even prayer impossible. And anyway, he didn't know any prayers to say; praying had never been much in his line. There was no doubt that this Jesus was God's king as he said he was, and that he would one day come again in all his kingly power. That was as certain as God himself, as certain as the fact of coming judgment.

Personally he had never thought much of kings, had never felt like obeying any of them. But a king who would pray forgiveness for the very men who were spiking his hands and feet to a cross . . . you could respect a king like that. He wouldn't mind being in his kingdom and obeying him. But what chance had he, a self-confessed anarchist, of being allowed so much as to enter his kingdom? And yet had he not prayed, 'Father, forgive them, for they know not what they do' (23:34)? If those soldiers could be forgiven because they had not realized exactly what they were doing, then certainly he hadn't realized before how wonderful God's king was. He hadn't meant to rebel against a king like that. 'Jesus,' he said, 'would you ever let me into your kingdom? Would you let me obey you? Lord, remember me when you come in your kingdom.'

And at once, to that poor broken rebel against man and God in the last few hours of his tortured life, there came clearly and without reserve that most kingly word from the King of kings himself: 'Assuredly, I say to you, today you will be with me in paradise.'

The Gospel *of the* Here *and* Hereafter

Center-point
of
Time

'For whoever is ashamed of me and of my words, of him will the Son of Man be ashamed when he comes in his glory and the glory of the Father and of the holy angels.

But I tell you truly, there are some standing here who will not taste death until they see the kingdom of God.'

Now about eight days after these sayings he took with him Peter and John and James and went up on the mountain to pray. And as he was praying, the appearance of his face was altered, and his clothing became dazzling white. And behold, two men were talking with him, Moses and Elijah, who appeared in glory and spoke of his departure, which he was about to accomplish at Jerusalem. Now Peter and those who were with him were heavy with sleep, but when they became fully awake they saw his glory and the two men who stood with him. And as the men were parting from him, Peter said to Jesus, 'Master, it is good that we are here. Let us make three tents, one for you and one for Moses and one for Elijah'—not knowing what he said.

As he was saying these things, a cloud came and overshadowed them, and they were afraid as they entered the cloud. And a voice came out of the cloud, saying, 'This is my Son, my Chosen One; listen to him!' And when the voice had spoken, Jesus was found alone. And they kept silent and told no one in those days anything of what they had seen.

Luke 9:26–36

Luke apparently was a medical doctor (Col 4:14), and here and there in his Gospel there are features that show the special interests of a physician. One such feature is Luke's interest in death.[1] In the course of his professional duties he would often have been obliged to stand by and watch a patient of his, in spite of all he could do for him, succumb to disease or old age; and although he doubtless became to some extent hardened to it, there must have been occasions when he fell to wondering about the significance of death. Was it the final catastrophe? Or was there something beyond? If so, what? And could people be certain about their destiny in the next world?

In Christ, Luke found the answers to all these questions, and it is understandable that he should want to tell the world what those answers were. Instead of the gloom and darkness and fear that surrounded death in the pagan world, and the uncertain personal hope of his Jewish contemporaries, he now knew the surge of triumph and confidence that they enjoy who have discovered that Christ 'abolished death and brought life and immortality to light through the gospel' (2 Tim 1:10). So in his Gospel he introduces us at every turn, in a way no other Gospel writer does, to people who are on the point of leaving this world for the next or else have just passed over.

Very early we meet the aged and saintly Simeon (Luke 2:25–35). It had been revealed to him, we are told, that he should not see death before he had seen the Lord's Christ; but on this occasion he saw him, and picking up the infant Jesus in his arms he said, 'Lord, now you are letting your servant depart in peace' (2:29). At the other end of his Gospel, Luke tells us of one of the bandits who were crucified along with Christ (23:39–43). In the very last moments of his life we see the man repent, trust the Saviour, and pass into the world beyond with the glorious promise of the Saviour ringing in his ears and heart, 'Today you will be with me in Paradise' (23:43).

---

[1] Another such feature, often remarked on by the commentators, is to be found in his account of Christ's healing of the woman who suffered from haemorrhage (Luke 8:43–47). Mark says of this woman that she 'had suffered much under many physicians, and had spent all that she had, and was no better but rather grew worse' (Mark 5:26). Apparently her doctors' fees had been as high as their treatment had been painful and ineffective. But Luke's account is briefer, less derogatory to the medical profession, and seems to put the blame for the woman's continued illness on the woman herself, or at least on the illness. He says simply, she 'had spent all her living on physicians, [and] she could not be healed by anyone' (Luke 8:43).

In his chapter 7, Luke tells us that on one occasion Christ was approaching the village of Nain, when he encountered a funeral procession: a broken-hearted widow was following the remains of her one and only son to the grave. Christ stopped the procession, touched the bier, restored the young man to life, and gave him back to his mother.

Chapter 8 records that in Capernaum on another occasion, Christ entered a home where the only daughter of the family, a little girl of twelve, lay dead. Outside the house the hired professional mourners were already filling the air with their weird, though heartless, wailings. Christ bade them be quiet, and with his famous remark, 'she is not dead but sleeping' (8:52), took the young child by the hand, raised her to life again and gave her back to her parents.

The end of life

Not all Luke's stories on this theme are equally happy, of course. In his day, as in ours, there were many people who refused to think of death, or to prepare for it. Ostrich-like, they put their heads in the sand of business or family life and tried to forget that death was coming. In so doing they emptied life itself of a good deal of its significance. Life is meant to be a journey to a goal. To neglect that goal, to try to banish from one's mind all thoughts of life's destination, may seem to the shallow-minded a good recipe for making the most of life while it lasts; but actually it debases life's journey into a meaningless and pointless wandering, and it fills the consequent eternity with disaster.

But it is not only unbelievers who need to be reminded of the reality of the world to come. Even those who have believed in Christ—for whom to depart this life is to be present with the Lord (Phil 1:23)— even these need to be helped to assess the life to come as a reality and to live their lives here in such a way that the carry-over from this life to the next shall be as great as possible. As Paul would put it, they need to learn to be 'storing up treasure for themselves as a good foundation for the future, so that they may take hold of that which is truly life' (see 1 Tim 6:17–19). So Luke inserts yet another parable of Christ's, the parable of the Unjust Steward (Luke 16:1–13). It exhorts believers to use their temporal assets, money, time, talents and the like for the future. They should not of course use them in order to obtain salvation, for that is a gift and cannot be purchased with any assets of ours. They should use them, however, that when these temporal assets come to their end and life here is done, they may find on the other side many people they helped in their spiritual progress by wise use of their assets in this life, and whose consequent gratitude they shall enjoy forever.

Now, all these stories and parables, except the story of Jairus's daughter, are found only in Luke's Gospel. They suggest a very strong interest in the subject of death and what lies beyond, and we shall study most of them in some detail in the course of these four chapters. But first we must examine in depth the central story of the Gospel, because at its heart and climax it too is concerned with the same subject.

From the literary point of view, the Gospel of Luke falls into two major parts, the second of which begins at 9:51. At this juncture, Luke tells us that the time for our Lord to return to heaven had nearly come, and therefore he set his face to go to Jerusalem. Up to this point Christ has, so to speak, been coming into our world and drawing ever nearer to us; from this point onwards, however, he is in process of leaving this world and going back where he came from. If, then, the watershed of the Gospel is 9:51, the last major story before the watershed stands at the literary centre of the book. That story is in fact the account of the Mount of Transfiguration: what happened there, and what followed on the descent from the mountain (9:28–50). Matthew and Mark also record the Transfiguration, but only Luke makes it the centrepiece of his Gospel.

And what a majestic centrepiece it makes! As Christ was praying, we are told, 'the appearance of his face was altered, and his clothing became dazzling white. And behold, two men were talking with him, Moses and Elijah, who appeared in glory' (9:29–31). But not only so: Luke, and only Luke, tells us the subject of the conversation that passed between our Lord and Moses and Elijah on that glorious occasion: they 'spoke of his departure, which he was about to accomplish at Jerusalem' (9:31). Just imagine it: amid all the glory and splendour of that exalted moment, the subject of the conversation was death.

The death of Christ

But it was not just anybody's death they were discussing; it was the death of Christ. The word for death that they had used was apparently not the ordinary word but one that meant a 'going out', an 'exodus', a 'departure'. And very fitting it was that it should be Moses and Elijah who were discussing it, for both of them had had remarkable exits from this world. Moses had died and God had buried him, 'but no one knows the place of his burial to this day' (Deut 34:6). Elijah had not passed through death, but had been carried up alive with horses and chariots of fire: 'And Elijah went up by a whirlwind into heaven' (2 Kgs 2:11).

Yet now they were discussing an exodus from this world so much more significant than theirs that it stood in altogether a different and unique category. The death of Christ was to be the death that should break the power of death. As the Letter to the Hebrews puts it: 'Since therefore the children share in flesh and blood, he himself likewise partook of the same things, that through death he might destroy the one who has the power of death, that is, the devil, and deliver all those who through fear of death were subject to lifelong slavery' (2:14–15).

Moreover, Christ's death was to take away from every believer not only the fear of death, but also its sting. 'The sting of death is sin', says Paul (1 Cor 15:56). The process of dying can be a very painful thing, and the moments of parting from our friends and loved ones can be agonizingly sorrowful. But death's real sting lies in neither of these things. It lies in sin. Conscience, as well as God's word, tells us that after death comes the judgment. Death therefore addresses us inescapably to the question, 'What will God say about my sin, and what will he do with me in consequence?'

It is useless our indulging in wishful thinking at this point and hoping that somehow after death our sins are forgotten, or that in some way or another they lose their significance and everything magically turns out all right in the end. That kind of thing only happens in fairy stories; real life is different. Sin matters. It is an offence against God's law. In that sense 'the power of sin is the law', as Paul puts it (1 Cor 15:56); that is, sin will never cease to matter unless God revokes his law. And he will never do that. Our Lord affirmed most solemnly, 'until heaven and earth pass away, not an iota, not a dot, will pass from the Law until all is accomplished' (Matt 5:18).

Therefore, however painful the attacks may be by which death demolishes our physical frame, its most painful sting is in its tail as it sends us to face God's throne. How could the sting ever be removed? The answer is by the atoning death and resurrection of Christ. The good news is, 'that Christ died for our sins in accordance with the

Scriptures, that he was buried, that he was raised on the third day in accordance with the Scriptures' (1 Cor 15:3–4). It is that 'God shows his love for us in that while we were still sinners, Christ died for us. Since, therefore, we have now been justified by his blood, much more shall we be saved by him from the wrath of God' (Rom 5:8–9).

It is interesting therefore to notice that on the Mount of Transfiguration Christ, Moses and Elijah spoke of the death of Christ as something he must 'accomplish' at Jerusalem. His death was no accident. It was not even, from this point of view, a disaster or a tragedy. It was deliberately planned and just as deliberately executed. 'No one takes [my life] from me,' said Christ on another occasion; 'but I lay it down of my own accord. I have authority to lay it down, and I have authority to take it up again' (John 10:18).

And from this point of view too, it is again significant that it should have been Moses and Elijah who were discussing his death. Moses was the giver of the law; Elijah was one of the most famous of the Old Testament prophets. But both the Old Testament Law and the Old Testament prophets had pointed forward to the coming of Christ and his atoning death. Luke subsequently tells us about two disciples three days after Christ's death who were walking home to Emmaus, dejected and disappointed because Jesus had died, and wondering whether after all he could be the Christ. 'Jesus himself drew near and went with them. . . . And he said to them, "O foolish ones, and slow of heart to believe all that the prophets have spoken! Was it not necessary that the Christ should suffer these things and enter into his glory?" And beginning with Moses and all the Prophets, he interpreted to them in all the Scriptures the things concerning himself' (see Luke 24:13–27).

Christ's death is the great centre-point of sacred history, indeed of all history. In Old Testament times all God's purposes moved forward to it; on its basis all God's purposes shall be eventually fulfilled.

Gateway *to* Eternity

'For whoever is ashamed of me and of my words, of him will the Son of Man be ashamed when he comes in his glory and the glory of the Father and of the holy angels.

But I tell you truly, there are some standing here who will not taste death until they see the kingdom of God.'

Now about eight days after these sayings he took with him Peter and John and James and went up on the mountain to pray. And as he was praying, the appearance of his face was altered, and his clothing became dazzling white. And behold, two men were talking with him, Moses and Elijah, who appeared in glory and spoke of his departure, which he was about to accomplish at Jerusalem. Now Peter and those who were with him were heavy with sleep, but when they became fully awake they saw his glory and the two men who stood with him. And as the men were parting from him, Peter said to Jesus, 'Master, it is good that we are here. Let us make three tents, one for you and one for Moses and one for Elijah'—not knowing what he said.

As he was saying these things, a cloud came and overshadowed them, and they were afraid as they entered the cloud. And a voice came out of the cloud, saying, 'This is my Son, my Chosen One; listen to him!' And when the voice had spoken, Jesus was found alone. And they kept silent and told no one in those days anything of what they had seen.

Luke 9:26–36

We have considered the significance of the fact that on the Mount of Transfiguration it was Moses and Elijah who appeared in glory and held conversation with Christ about his death; and we must stay with that theme a little longer. Unlike Moses the Lawgiver, Elijah wrote very little. He is chiefly remembered for his famous trial of strength with the prophets of Baal on Mount Carmel (1 Kgs 18). The issue at stake on that momentous occasion was: 'Who is the true God? Baal or Jehovah?'

The criterion that both Elijah and the false prophets agreed upon by which to settle the dispute was that they should both build altars and prepare sacrifices upon them; and then the God who answered by sending down fire from heaven to consume the sacrifice should be regarded as the true God. The false prophets called aloud on Baal to hear them, and in their devotion cut themselves with knives and danced round their altar. But the fire did not come; there was not even a voice to answer them.

Then it was Elijah's turn. He first had the sacrifice and the altar heavily doused with water, to make it evident that there was to be no trickery in what should happen. Then simply and publicly he called on God to vindicate his name and to demonstrate his divine reality; and immediately there fell from heaven a fire that consumed the sacrifice, the wood, the water, and the very stones of the altar.

Long centuries have passed since then, but the greatest, the ultimate, question that every man and woman has to decide remains the same. Is there a God? Religions by the hundred claim that there is; but can you trust religion? Is it anything more than wishful thinking at best, and a load of old superstition at worst? And do not many religions quarrel among themselves, each claiming to be the right one and contradicting the others? How then can anyone be sure that the claim of Jesus Christ to be the unique Son of God is indeed true?

The question is basically the same as in Elijah's day, and so is the answer; and it turns on the question of sacrifice rather than morality. In the first place, all serious religions would agree on the importance of moral values. They would, so to speak, agree with Moses; though, if one may digress for a moment, when one compares Moses' law with the systems contemporary with him, one cannot help noticing how immeasurably superior his law is to theirs. At a time when all other nations were sunk in the crassest of idolatry, Moses alone preached an exalted monotheism. Besides that, Moses' law insisted that morality was an integral part of religion, whereas in many cultures religion was simply an elaborate system of currying favour with the gods, or at least of averting their wrath, and had little if anything to do with morality. So long as you kept up your sacrifices to the god who particularly favoured you, he could be expected to champion your cause, no matter how you treated your fellow men and women.

But to return from our digression: the ancient religions would have agreed in principle with Moses' insistence on the importance of morality, and so would most modern religions. Few would allege that morality does not matter at all. To say that murder, rape, lying, cheating and greed are all right, is to vote for social suicide. If therefore you compare religions on the basis of morality, certainly you will be able to say that some are better than others. But it will generally be simply a matter of degree because basically they all say the same.

An adequate sacrifice

The general agreement on morality leads us to a difficulty that only Christ can answer. If sin matters, and matters absolutely, on what grounds can anyone be forgiven? Forgiveness that sets aside the sanctions of the moral law, and agrees simply and conveniently to forget the sin, in effect denies the moral law and admits that sin does not matter much after all. On the other hand, to insist on the absolute sanctions of the law is to consign us all to disaster, for we have all broken that law. To this fundamental dilemma mere morality has no solution, even if the morality in question is the law of Moses or the Sermon on the Mount.

Let Elijah, first on Mount Carmel and then on the Mount of Transfiguration, point us to the solution. It is to be found in the true sacrifice accepted by God, and that sacrifice is the death of Christ. For when Elijah prepared the sacrifice on Mount Carmel, there came down fire from heaven before the astonished eyes of the people, and acknowledged the sacrifice as the God-given means by which a guilty people could be reconciled to God. So at the Transfiguration, when Elijah and Moses had discussed with Christ his forthcoming death and sacrifice, there came a cloud and overshadowed the whole mountain, and a voice from the cloud said, 'This is my Son, my Chosen One; listen to him!' (Luke 9:35).

We need to grasp the full significance of this, for at first the three apostles didn't. Overwhelmed by the grandeur of the occasion, Peter reacted by suggesting that they should be allowed to make three tents, one for Jesus, one for Moses, and one for Elijah. He meant no insult to Christ; indeed, he may have felt that he was paying Christ great honour. But inadvertently he was putting Christ on the same level as Moses and Elijah, and the divine voice from the cloud gently rebuked him. A Christ that was just another Moses or Elijah, or even a Christ that was superior to Moses and Elijah but in the same category, would be no use to us in our dilemma. Moses and Elijah, for all their greatness as inspired lawgiver and prophet, were sinners themselves. All the great religious leaders of the world have without exception been sinners likewise, and the holier they have been, the more readily they have acknowledged it and emphasized the vast gap that separates the holiest of mere men from the absolute holiness of God. Jesus Christ was sinless, as sinless as God himself; he was and is God's Son.

But more. Had the Son of God come among us as the supreme exponent of morality and lived a sinless life himself in accordance with his own teaching and done nothing more, still he would not have solved our dilemma. He would simply have done, though perfectly, what all other religious leaders have done to their limited extent, namely, increased our awareness of sin and therefore the burden of our guilt.

But Christ did more than this, and in doing it not only solved our dilemma but showed himself utterly unique and altogether different from all others. He came in order deliberately to die, to accomplish a death at Jerusalem in which, as the Son of God and one with the Father, he might bear the sanctions of the divine law that he himself had promulgated, and give himself as a ransom for all. His death has secured redemption and made forgiveness possible, not by bending the law or by saying that sin does not really matter very much after all, but by righteously upholding the law and by honouring its sanctions to the very limit, so that, as Scripture puts it, God can be just and at the same time the justifier of the one who believes in Jesus (Rom 3:26).

Christ is unique

His death solves our dilemma, but at the same time, as I have said, it proclaims Christ as unique. No other religious leader or philosopher in the course of the whole of known human history has ever entered our world heralded by prophets like Moses and Elijah and the rest of the Jewish seers. No other has ever entered announcing that he had come primarily to give himself to God as a ransom for the sins of the world. On this point of fundamental importance and paramount significance there is no question of judging between the claim of Christ and anybody else: only Christ has ever made the claim. And we may know that it is true, as a person knows bread is true, for it satisfies hunger, and water true because it satisfies thirst. So we may know that the claim of Christ is true: the death of God's Son as the God-given sacrifice for the sins of the world satisfies the fundamental problem of the human situation as nothing else does or can.

So then the central topic of conversation on the mountain of transfiguration was the death of Christ. But there was nothing gloomy about the occasion. Quite the opposite, all was radiantly glorious. The aspect of Christ's face was changed, we are told, and his clothing became brilliant as lightning. Moses and Elijah too appeared in glory. This was no occasion for grief or mourning. Some days earlier, Christ had promised his disciples that they would not see death before they saw the kingdom of God (Luke 9:27); and now on the Mount of Transfiguration they were evidently being given the promised foreview of that coming kingdom. Let us notice its leading features.

The kingdom

First of all, the appearance of Moses and Elijah together—when their lives in this world had been separated by centuries—shows that in that kingdom time is annihilated. After all the centuries which separated them from Christ in this world, that they should be living together with him in that kingdom, and still be recognizable as Moses and Elijah, demonstrates that in that world people survive not as impersonal spirit but as distinct personalities.

Then let us observe again what we noticed earlier, that Moses and Elijah had entered that eternal world in different ways. Moses had died and been buried; Elijah had not died but had been taken up alive into heaven. And in this feature too we may discern a foreview of what shall happen on a far grander scale in the first resurrection at the second coming of Christ. Twice in his letters Paul describes the order of events at the second coming; and on each occasion he emphasizes the fact that, while believers who have died will be raised again, believers who are still alive when the Lord comes will be taken up into heaven without dying. Here are the passages:

> For this we declare to you by a word from the Lord, that we who are alive, who are left until the coming of the Lord, will not precede those who have fallen asleep. For the Lord himself will descend from heaven with a cry of command, with the voice of an archangel, and with the sound of the trumpet of God. And the dead in Christ will rise first. Then we who are alive, who are left, will be caught up together with them in the clouds to meet the Lord in the air, and so we will always be with the Lord. (1 Thess 4:15–17)

> I tell you this, brothers: flesh and blood cannot inherit the kingdom of God, nor does the perishable inherit the imperishable. Behold! I tell you a mystery. We shall not all sleep, but we shall all be changed, in a moment, in the twinkling of an eye, at the last trumpet. For the trumpet will sound, and the dead will be raised imperishable, and we shall be changed. (1 Cor 15:50–52)

But another most significant thing that happened on the Mount of Transfiguration was the transfiguration of Christ himself. Inasmuch as he was the Son of God, it is nothing to be wondered at if on that occasion the overflowing of his essential glory should have transformed his human body. But he was not only divine, he was human too; so that, as the astonished disciples beheld the mysterious transfiguration of his body, they were doubtless being given a foreview of the glorious body that Christ should receive in resurrection. And not only Christ; believers are assured that, whether they enter the world to come through death and resurrection, or without dying are caught up to meet the Lord when he comes, they shall all be changed.

> But our citizenship is in heaven, and from it we await a Saviour, the Lord Jesus Christ, who will transform our lowly body to be like his glorious body, by the power than enables him even to subject all things to himself. (Phil 3:20–21)

This is stupendously marvellous; but it is not unreasonable, nor yet a fairy story. Even in this world, argues Paul in 1 Corinthians 15, the material called flesh exists in many forms. There is the flesh of animals, the flesh of fish, the flesh of birds, as well as human flesh. They are all flesh but they are all different, as we know from the great difficulties scientists have faced in trying to make animal organs suitable for transplantation into human beings. If then in this world flesh can exist in different forms, it is not difficult to accept that human flesh, which has one form in this world, will exist in a different form in the world to come and yet still be human.

Or take another analogy, says Paul. The beautiful, many-grained ear of wheat that rises from the well-tilled field is a vastly different thing from the bare grain that was earlier sown in the ground and from which it grew. But it is still wheat. So it is with the bodies of believers who have died and are raised, and with the bodies of those believers who without dying are transformed at the second coming of Christ. They will be glorified bodies, but they will be real bodies and human still.

One final point, to be fair to Scripture and to ourselves. If we ask Scripture who they are that shall share the eternal glory of Christ at his second coming, the reply invariably comes back: those that are in Christ, or those that are Christ's. For instance, 1 Thessalonians 4:16 says that at the first resurrection not all the dead, but 'the dead in Christ' will rise. And 1 Corinthians 15:23 similarly says that 'at his coming those who belong to Christ' shall be made alive. Again, the immediately preceding verse mentions two categories: 'For as in Adam all die, so also in Christ shall all be made alive' (1 Cor 15:22). Now, it is clear enough that we all belong to the first category simply by having been born into this world. But the New Testament everywhere affirms that all in the first category are not automatically included in the second. It would surely be prudent to discover from the New Testament how to get into this second category, and then of course to get into it.

When *we* Cross Over

Now there was a man in Jerusalem, whose name was Simeon, and this man was righteous and devout, waiting for the consolation of Israel, and the Holy Spirit was upon him. And it had been revealed to him by the Holy Spirit that he would not see death before he had seen the Lord's Christ. And he came in the Spirit into the temple, and when the parents brought in the child Jesus, to do for him according to the custom of the Law, he took him up in his arms and blessed God and said,

> 'Lord, now you are letting your servant depart in peace, according to your word; for my eyes have seen your salvation that you have prepared in the presence of all peoples, a light for revelation to the Gentiles, and for glory to your people Israel.'

And his father and his mother marvelled at what was said about him. And Simeon blessed them and said to Mary his mother, 'Behold, this child is appointed for the fall and rising of many in Israel, and for a sign that is opposed (and a sword will pierce through your own soul also), so that thoughts from many hearts may be revealed.'

Luke 2:25–35

One of the criminals who were hanged railed at him, saying, 'Are you not the Christ? Save yourself and us!'

But the other rebuked him, saying, 'Do you not fear God, since you are under the same sentence of condemnation? And we indeed justly, for we are receiving the due reward of our deeds; but this man has done nothing wrong.'

And he said, 'Jesus, remember me when you come into your kingdom.'

And he said to him, 'Truly, I say to you, today you will be with me in Paradise.'

Luke 23:39–43

For some considerable time on the Mount of Transfiguration Christ, Moses and Elijah had been discussing the death that Christ was to accomplish at Jerusalem. To anyone who had been listening, it would have been perfectly clear that Christ was going away, but for the greater part of the conversation Peter and the other two disciples had been asleep. Perhaps the mystery and the awesome brilliance of the occasion had been more than their mortal flesh could endure. At any rate they fell asleep.

At length the conversation was over, and Moses and Elijah were getting ready to depart, when Peter suddenly woke up. Understandably he felt deeply embarrassed, and to cover his confusion he attempted to make a remark. 'Master,' said he, 'it is good that we are here. Let us make three tents, one for you and one for Moses and one for Elijah' (9:33). Luke adds that Peter did not realize what he was saying. Obviously not, since the whole conversation had been about Christ's going away, and Peter suggested staying put.

Life's journey

We may smile at Peter, but we often appear to be saying the same thing—not of course in so many words, but by the way we live. We know that the Bible declares that life is a journey to an eternal heaven—or hell; we have heard it many times. But we live as though we are going to stay here forever, as though this life is everything and there is no eternal goal. Of course, Peter's remark was very understandable. The life of a Galilean fisherman was hard and humdrum; so when a rare occasion of splendour and enchantment came his way, it was only natural that he should want to make it last as long as possible.

Nor is there anything necessarily wrong with his or our desire to enjoy life to the full and to pack as much interest and adventure into it as possible. If life has an eternal goal, then every step of the journey has eternal significance. And if the goal is to be enjoyed, that is no reason why the journey should not be enjoyed as well. Most of us enjoy travelling as well as arriving. We love to get into the cockpit with the pilots, or onto the bridge with the captain, to see all there is to be seen out of the windows, to explore every port of call.

On the other hand, if while sailing from America to Ireland the captain of the vessel presently forgot he was on a journey, and simply steered the ship in never-ending circles round the middle of the Atlantic instead of making for the destination, most of the passengers in the ship would eventually become disenchanted with the voyage. And the danger is that in our effort to enjoy this life to the full, we lose sight of the goal, and thereby defeat the very object that we set out to achieve. We rob this life of its eternal, and therefore of its most important and enjoyable, dimension. We cease travelling and begin meandering through life, and all this at the peril of arriving in eternity utterly unprepared.

Perhaps this is why the Bible, unlike a good deal of popular preaching, very seldom uses the phrase 'go to heaven', but constantly urges us to receive eternal life now. For eternal life is not a something that we must wait until we get to heaven before we receive it; it is an added, eternal dimension to this life, which is enjoyed by those who enter now into a personal relationship with the eternal God through Jesus Christ. Of course, since it springs from a relationship that is eternal, it continues unbroken when the temporary phase of life in this world is done. But the relationship must be entered into in this life, if it is to exist in the next; hence the danger of becoming so preoccupied with the temporary side of this life that we fail to lay hold of the eternal.

So then, Christ allowed his disciples to stay long enough on the Mount of Transfiguration to get a foreview of his eternal kingdom and to become convinced of its reality. It made an indelible impression on Peter. Writing years later towards the end of his life, in order to urge his fellow Christians to prepare well for their entrance 'into the eternal kingdom of our Lord and Saviour Jesus Christ' (2 Pet 1:11), he remarks that his own death is near. Significantly, the word he uses, 'decease,' is the word 'exodus'—the very word that Luke uses in recording the conversation on the mount.

And then Peter adds:

> For we did not follow cleverly devised myths when we made known to you the power and coming of our Lord Jesus Christ, but we were eyewitnesses of his majesty. For when he received honour and glory from God the Father, and the voice was borne to him by the Majestic Glory, 'This is my beloved Son, with whom I am well pleased', we ourselves heard this very voice borne from heaven, for we were with him on the holy mountain. (2 Pet 1:16–18)

But as soon as the lesson of the transfiguration was learnt, Christ took his disciples down the mountain, and, as the trailblazer, began the journey that should lead him via suffering and death at Jerusalem to heaven (Luke 9:51).

Start of the journey

Suppose then we take Christ seriously, and Peter seriously, and determine to set out on the journey that leads to God's heaven. Two questions naturally arise. The first is: Where does the journey start? The answer is simple and may be given in Peter's own words. He describes the goal as 'an inheritance that is imperishable, undefiled, and unfading, kept in heaven for you' (1 Pet 1:4). Then he describes the start of the spiritual pilgrimage that leads to the goal: 'since you have been born again, not of perishable seed but of imperishable, through the living and abiding word of God . . .' (1:23). In other words, the journey begins when we first receive the word of God and personally trust the Saviour, and are born again as newborn babies into the family of God.

The second question is: Can we be sure that, having started out on the journey, we shall arrive in God's heaven, and not miss our way and end up disastrously elsewhere? The straight and certain answer to this question is: Yes, we can be sure! Let Luke answer this time. Very early in his narrative of the journey, Luke tells us about an occasion when the disciples came to Christ elated and overjoyed at the success they had had at casting out demons in his name. He replied, 'Nevertheless, do not rejoice in this, that the spirits are subject to you, but rejoice that your names are written in heaven' (Luke 10:20).

So here was assurance that, as they journeyed through life, they were already registered as citizens of heaven—as men whose fatherland is heaven, and who by the grace of God have citizens' right to be in the heavenly city. This may strike some people as strange, since popular thinking about theology has put it about that none of us can be certain of heaven until we get there (if we ever do) and that for some to say they are certain is plain presumption.

But the fact is that not only did the apostles receive this assurance from the Lord. The early Christians all enjoyed this same assurance— the rank and file, if one may use the term simply to contrast them with spiritual giants like the apostles. Paul, in the Letter to the Philippians for instance, in the course of other things, makes an aside that is very revealing. He is in process of asking one of his friends at Philippi to help some of his fellow-workers when he says:

> Yes, I ask you also, true companion, help these women, who have laboured side by side with me in the gospel together with Clement and the rest of my fellow workers, whose names are in the book of life. (Phil 4:3)

The almost casual way in which Paul adds this remark, that their names are written in the book of life, shows quite clearly that he was not propounding something new that they did not already know. They had known and enjoyed this assurance ever since they had first trusted Christ. They knew themselves as men and women whose names were enrolled in the citizen lists of heaven. Only a few verses earlier Paul had reminded them, 'our citizenship is in heaven' (3:20).

Certainty of arrival

This is obviously important, but it is even more important than some of us might have noticed. According to Revelation 20:11–15, which describes the final judgment, the sole criterion by which it is decided whether anyone shall be received into God's heaven or banished to the lake of fire is whether or not their name is 'found written in the book of life' (v. 15). It is true that those who are banished are judged 'according to what they had done' (v. 12), for the lost are not all given one single undifferentiated sentence, but in God's justice 'it will be more bearable' for some in the day of judgment than for others, because they had less light and opportunity (see Luke 10:14).

But the basic question of whether anyone shall be banished or received into heaven is not to be decided on the ground of works at all. If heaven were entered on the ground of our works and merit, none of us would ever enter. Entry there is given as a gift to all whose names are written in the book of life, and is denied to none except those whose names are not found written in the book of life.

If we ask on what terms and conditions anyone's name is written in that book, it is answer enough if we notice that the book of life is elsewhere described as the Lamb's book of life (Rev 13:8). This book is the record of all who have trusted Christ as the Lamb of God; of all who are covered by his infinite sacrifice for sin. For the blood of Jesus Christ, God's Son, cleanses from all sin, removes all guilt and purchases for the believer the citizen-rights of heaven. It is, then, of the utmost importance that we should be sure that we are personally trusting in the Lamb of God, in him and in nothing else, and that our names are written in his book of life.

But if we feel that all this is too good to be true, let us get back to the Gospel of Luke and study closely two men who are described there. Both are nearing the end of life's journey and are about to cross over into God's great eternity. Both are filled with confidence and assurance. What is the ground of their assurance?

An elderly saint

The one man is Simeon: his story is given in Luke 2:25–35. Simeon had lived a long life of consistent devotion to God and of practical righteousness, and now as a mature saint he was coming like a golden sheaf to the great harvest home. Evidently he lived in the closest intimacy with God, for God had revealed to him that he should not see death until he had seen the Lord's Christ. Coming into the temple one day, he saw Mary and Joseph with the baby Jesus. Immediately he recognized in the baby the very Saviour of whose coming God had told him; and in the same instant he realized that his own days on earth were now soon to be at an end.

There followed a wonderful scene, as the aged saint gently lifted the child from Mary, 'took him up in his arms and blessed God and said: "Lord, now you are letting your servant depart in peace, according to your word; for my eyes have seen your salvation"' (2:28–30). What a wonderful picture he makes as he stands there with the babe in his arms, his white hair and his noble face radiant already with the glory of eternity, like a mountain peak lit up by the rays of the rising sun! And what wonderful stories he could tell, if he had the mind, about his long life: stories of great spiritual achievements, of diligent and sometimes rapturous prayer, of missions of mercy, of noble good works.

But there is no word of such things now. The man is facing eternity, about to make his exodus from this world, and he is declaring how it is he can enter eternity in peace. There is therefore not a word about his own life; his eyes are resting solely on the life of another. 'My eyes have seen your salvation', he exclaims. We have no need to ask where. He is gazing intently at the Christ. True, he was not thinking selfishly of himself alone: here was a salvation big enough for all peoples and nations. But a salvation big enough for all mankind was big enough for Simeon. He needed nothing more; he had Christ.

As we turn to leave him, notice his arms. He stands there not holding Christ in one arm and grasping something else in the other. He has not only personally received Christ, but he is holding nothing else: both his arms are round Christ. Therein is the secret of his peace. And when our time comes to cross over, we too may go in profound and utter peace, if for our salvation we have personally received the Saviour and are depending on nothing but him.

A dying criminal

The other man is the so-called dying thief. His story is told in 23:39–43. There could not be a greater contrast than that between this man and Simeon. His past held no good works worth mentioning: he was a self-confessed criminal, bandit and murderer, and he was now receiving what he described as the due reward of his deeds. Moreover, there was no possibility of his undertaking to make amends in the future, for he had no future on this earth. Like Simeon, though in vastly different circumstances, he was standing on the brink of eternity and was about to cross over. How could such a man ever hope to depart in peace? And yet he did. For in the last few hours of his life he turned in true repentance and trusted the Saviour. He went into eternity in complete assurance and peace based on the unbreakable word of Christ, 'today you will be with me in Paradise' (23:43).

Luke's message is clear. Whether we are Simeons or criminals, or neither but somewhere in between the two extremes, we too can be certain of our destiny. We can journey towards it with confident assurance and arrive at last in peace, if in genuine repentance we put our trust solely in the person, the work and the word of Christ.

STORY EIGHT

Over
on the
Other
Side

While he was still speaking, someone from the ruler's house came and said, 'Your daughter is dead; do not trouble the Teacher any more.'

But Jesus on hearing this answered him, 'Do not fear; only believe, and she will be well.'

And when he came to the house, he allowed no one to enter with him, except Peter and John and James, and the father and mother of the child. And all were weeping and mourning for her, but he said, 'Do not weep, for she is not dead but sleeping.'

And they laughed at him, knowing that she was dead. But taking her by the hand he called, saying, 'Child, arise.' And her spirit returned, and she got up at once. And he directed that something should be given to her to eat. And her parents were amazed, but he charged them to tell no one what had happened.

Luke 8:49–56

Someone in the crowd said to him, 'Teacher, tell my brother to divide the inheritance with me.'

But he said to him, 'Man, who made me a judge or arbitrator over you?' And he said to them, 'Take care, and be on your guard against all covetousness, for one's life does not consist in the abundance of one's possessions.'

And he told them a parable, saying, 'The land of a rich man produced plentifully, and he thought to himself, "What shall I do, for I have nowhere to store my crops?"

And he said, "I will do this: I will tear down my barns and build larger ones, and there I will store all my grain and my goods. And I will say to my soul, Soul, you have ample goods laid up for many years; relax, eat, drink, be merry."

But God said to him, "Fool! This night your soul is required of you, and the things you have prepared, whose will they be?"

So is the one who lays up treasure for himself and is not rich towards God.'

Luke 12:13–21

He also said to the disciples, 'There was a rich man who had a manager, and charges were brought to him that this man was wasting his possessions. And he called him and said to him, "What is this that I hear about you? Turn in the account of your management, for you can no longer be manager."

And the manager said to himself, "What shall I do, since my master is taking the management away from me? I am not strong enough to dig, and I am ashamed to beg. I have decided what to do, so that when I am removed from management, people may receive me into their houses."

So, summoning his master's debtors one by one, he said to the first, "How much do you owe my master?"

He said, "A hundred measures of oil."

He said to him, "Take your bill, and sit down quickly and write fifty."

Then he said to another, "And how much do you owe?"

He said, "A hundred measures of wheat."

He said to him, "Take your bill, and write eighty."

The master commended the dishonest manager for his shrewdness. For the sons of this world are more shrewd in dealing with their own generation than the sons of light. And I tell you, make friends for yourselves by means of unrighteous wealth, so that when it fails they may receive you into the eternal dwellings.

'One who is faithful in a very little is also faithful in much, and one who is dishonest in a very little is also dishonest in much. If then you have not been faithful with the unrighteous wealth, who will entrust to you the true riches? And if you have not been faithful with that which is another's, who will give you that which is your own?

No servant can serve two masters, for either he will hate the one and love the other, or he will be devoted to the one and despise the other. You cannot serve God and money.'

Luke 16:1–13

There was a rich man who was clothed in purple and fine linen and who feasted sumptuously every day. And at his gate was laid a poor man named Lazarus, covered with sores, who desired to be fed with what fell from the rich man's table. Moreover, even the dogs came and licked his sores.

The poor man died and was carried by the angels to Abraham's side. The rich man also died and was buried, and in Hades, being in torment, he lifted up his eyes and saw Abraham far off and Lazarus at his side. And he called out, 'Father Abraham, have mercy on me, and send Lazarus to dip the end of his finger in water and cool my tongue, for I am in anguish in this flame.'

But Abraham said, 'Child, remember that you in your lifetime received your good things, and Lazarus in like manner bad things; but now he is comforted here, and you are in anguish. And besides all this, between us and you a great chasm has been fixed, in order that those who would pass from here to you may not do so, and none may cross from there to us.'

And he said, 'Then I beg you, father, to send him to my father's house— for I have five brothers—so that he may warn them, lest they also come into this place of torment.'

But Abraham said, 'They have Moses and the Prophets; let them hear them.'

And he said, 'No, father Abraham, but if someone goes to them from the dead, they will repent.'

He said to him, 'If they do not hear Moses and the Prophets, neither will they be convinced if someone should rise from the dead.'

Luke 16:19–31

At this point in our studies, the question may well arise: where then are the dead, and in what state are they? Let us take first 'the dead in Christ' as the New Testament calls them (1 Thess 4:16), that is, people who in this life enter into a personal relationship with Christ, and subsequently die. Scripture teaches that upon death they go to be with Christ. We see this from our Lord's words to the dying thief: 'Today you will be with me in Paradise' (Luke 23:43).

And Paul uses the same phrase when he speaks of the matter. In Philippians 1:23, he confesses to having a desire to 'depart and be with Christ'. Similarly in 2 Corinthians 5:6–8, he says: 'We know that while we are at home in the body we are away from the Lord, . . . Yes, we are of good courage, and we would rather be away from the body and at home with the Lord.'

Moreover, it would appear from our Lord's words to the dying thief that the believer goes to be with Christ immediately upon death without any interval. 'Today', said our Lord, 'you will be with me in Paradise.' The same impression is conveyed by what Scripture says of the state of the departed believer. In the story of Lazarus, who died before our Lord himself died and rose again, we are told that 'the poor man died and was carried by the angels to Abraham's side', i.e. he was taken into the company of the believing (Luke 16:22–25).

And as to his state we are further told that 'he is comforted'. In life he had been tormented by illness and poverty; now his suffering was all at an end—he was comforted. Similarly with the dying thief; only the situation was different in this respect, that the Saviour himself was about to die and enter the world beyond: 'Today you will be with me in Paradise,' said Christ. The word paradise originally meant a pleasure garden, and it is used in the Septuagint translation of the Old Testament to describe the garden of Eden before sin entered with its train of consequent pain and sorrow. When therefore it is used in the New Testament of the world beyond, as it is in Luke 23:43; 2 Corinthians 12:3; Revelation 2:7, it is evident that it implies a state in which there is no more pain or sorrow.

Paul's remarks on the subject agree with this. He says in Philippians 1:23 that to be with Christ is very far better, i.e. far better than anything he had ever known or experienced here on earth. We should remember at this point that Paul's experiences of Christ even in this life had been exceedingly intimate and direct; yet when he thinks of what it would mean to leave the body and depart to be with Christ, he says the difference would be the difference between being away in exile and being at home.

With Christ

Now, in all this it is interesting to notice that the dominant element in the departed believer's bliss is everywhere described as personal nearness to Christ. And this emphasis is maintained in those Scriptures which speak of our Lord's second coming, the bodily resurrection of the dead and the transformation of the living. Says Christ of that event: 'I will come again and will take you to myself, that where I am you may be also' (John 14:3); and again, 'Father, I desire that they also, whom you have given me, may be with me where I am, to see my glory' (17:24). Similarly, Paul says in concluding his account of the first resurrection: 'Then we who are alive, who are left, will be caught up together with them in the clouds to meet the Lord in the air, and so we will always be with the Lord' (1 Thess 4:17).

But if the spirits of the departed believers are with Christ until the resurrection, Scripture also says their bodies are asleep. In Luke 8:49–56, for instance, we have described the death of Jairus's daughter. The wailing of the professional mourners outside the house was meant to express the sorrow of the relatives and the sympathy of their friends. When Christ came and said, 'Do not weep, for she is not dead but sleeping,' the wailing suddenly ceased and turned to mocking laughter: for here were people who had no faith and utterly no hope or real comfort. The best they could do was to offer the relatives help to work the emotions of grief out of their system by wild and deliberate wailings, so that they would not bottle up their grief and bring harmful psychosomatic effects on themselves later on in life. But their professionalism knew nothing of positive comfort or hope; and what is more, it resented the possible loss of income that would result if the parents received Christ's message of hope and found it to be true.

'She is not dead but sleeping', said the Saviour (8:52). And then he took her by the hand and raised her up. Since then Christians have been helped to dry their tears by the knowledge that, though sleep is not the highest mode of life, it is not the ultimate, or even a permanent, disaster. And for bodies that are worn out and spent, sleep is for the time being the happiest thing. So Paul describes the Christian dead as 'those who have fallen asleep' (1 Thess 4:14); and the English word 'cemetery', though now a cold and cheerless word, once bore its witness to the Christian faith: it is a word borrowed directly from Greek and means 'a place where people sleep'.

Without Christ

What, then, of those who die unbelieving and unrepentant? This is a most distressing topic and one that any sensitive person would prefer not to discuss. But we would be dishonest and disloyal to ourselves if we attempted to evade it. What we know of the matter is largely told us by our Lord himself, and it will help us if we recall that, when he looked over Jerusalem and thought of even the temporal disasters that were to overtake the city because of its people's sin and refusal of salvation, he broke down and wept. And the Saviour who died so that all men and women—whether they have heard of him or not—might have the opportunity to be saved if only they repent and in true faith cast themselves on the mercy of God, can be trusted to do nothing inconsistent with perfect love when he comes to judge.

Luke records, then, the story our Lord told about a certain beggar Lazarus and an unnamed rich man, in which our Lord solemnly affirmed that:

> The rich man also died and was buried, and in Hades, being in torment, he lifted up his eyes and saw Abraham far off and Lazarus at his side. And he called out, 'Father Abraham, have mercy on me, and send Lazarus to dip the end of his finger in water and cool my tongue, for I am in anguish in this flame.' But Abraham said, 'Child, remember that you in your lifetime received your good things, and Lazarus in like manner bad things; but now he is comforted here, and you are in anguish. And besides all this, between us and you a great chasm has been fixed, in order that those who would pass from here to you may not do so, and none may cross from there to us.' (Luke 16:22–26)

A factual description

Before we can draw the main lesson from this story, we must first examine two considerations that, it is sometimes alleged, make it improper to use the details of the story as evidence for the state of the impenitent after death. In the first place some maintain that the story is a parable, and therefore its details cannot be taken as factually true. But to say this is to confuse our Lord's parables with fables.

Fables are perfectly respectable means of conveying truth, and occasionally they are to be found in Scripture (e.g. Jotham's fable in Judges 9). But in fables, things are represented as happening which never take place in real life: birds talk, animals speak, the sun holds an argument with the wind, and so forth. Therefore, certainly one could not take the circumstantial details of fables like this as reliable evidence for ornithology, zoology and meteorology.

But none of the stories told by our Lord are fables, though many are parables. And in his parables the circumstantial detail is always and without exception true to real life, though serving to convey a higher spiritual lesson. For instance, in the parable of the Wheat and Tares the wheat represents the sons of the kingdom and the tares stand for the sons of the evil one. And yet the details of wheat and tares are at their basic level true to life: actual farmers do sow literal wheat in very tangible fields and unfortunately on the very best of farms there are such things as weeds.

The story of the rich man and Lazarus may then be a parable conveying some higher spiritual meaning (though what higher meaning it could convey beyond what it literally says is difficult to see); but even so that would be no reason for supposing that its details are not true to life. And added to this is the consideration that Luke in recording the story does not say that it is a parable. Indeed, if it were a parable it would be the only parable among the many parables Christ told in which a character is named.

The second objection to taking the details of the story as a guide to the state of the impenitent dead would, if put in an extreme form, run something like this: some of the details in the description are obviously not literal, therefore we need not suppose that any of it is real. But this is very shallow reasoning. Certainly some of the descriptions are given in metaphorical language, but that does not mean they are not describing something real. When it says that the beggar was carried into Abraham's bosom, it obviously does not intend us to picture him being dandled on Abraham's lap like a baby. But the fact that the phrase is metaphorical and not literal does nothing to diminish the literal reality of the fellowship that he now enjoyed with Abraham and the saints.

If I were to complain that a certain part of my body was inflamed, no one would take me to mean that someone had set light to my body and that it was now in flames. But on the other hand, none would deny that there was a very real and painful burning going on in my flesh. And so, when the rich man complains that he is being tormented in a flame, it is not necessary to think that the flame was of the literal kind that we see in our coal fires. Indeed, seeing his sins were spiritual and mental, it is likely that his anguish also would be spiritual and mental.

Even so, we must be careful before we deny that there would be any physical element in his suffering. In this life, mental and spiritual anguish very commonly affect our bodies as well as our minds, and induce physical unease and pain; and we should be very rash to assert that what happens here could not possibly happen there. If Christ has spoken to us about the other world in metaphors, we may rest assured that those metaphors were chosen because they convey to us what the realities of that world are like, better than any other form of expression.

How to prepare

We must then be very careful not to fall into the temptation of taking what the Bible says about the world to come less than absolutely seriously. Indeed, it was taking it less than seriously that eventually landed the rich man in hell. It is very important to see that he was not sent there because he was rich, but because of his unbelief, as the end of the story makes abundantly clear. That unbelief manifested itself in the way he treated his poor neighbour. The Bible told him that he was to love his neighbour as himself and he didn't make the slightest attempt to do so.

But behind his failure to love his neighbour was a deeper unbelief that, while outwardly perhaps professing to believe the Bible as the word of God, did not take it seriously to mean what it said. Evidently the man thought that, though the Bible laid down its moral demands and warned that they were absolute, he could live all his life paying them no serious attention and yet after death things would somehow turn out all right. Listen to the man pleading with Abraham. He asks that Lazarus should be sent from the dead to warn his brothers who were still on earth, so that they would not come to the place of torment.

Abraham replies that there is no need to send Lazarus, because his brothers have Moses and the Prophets. 'Yes, I know they have,' says the rich man, 'but . . .' The 'but' is very revealing: he too in life had had Moses and the Prophets, and had probably professed to believe them. But he hadn't really believed them at all, and he knew that his brothers didn't really believe them either. 'If one goes to them from the dead', he suggested, 'they will repent.' But it is more likely that they would have dismissed the apparition as a bad dream, or as imagination, or as something that science could, or would soon be able to, explain away.

No, said Abraham, the brothers will get no ghostly visitations; for if they do not believe the Bible, neither will they be persuaded if one rose from the dead. There are no gimmicks in God's message to men. He appeals to our moral judgment, not to our ghoulish curiosity. If our moral judgment is so perverse that it can neglect and disregard the plain moral warnings of God's word as being irrelevant and not worthy of serious attention, our sickness is worse than the seeing of any number of ghosts would cure.

Wasted treasure

Two parables in Luke remain for our consideration. Both parables urge those who believe in the reality of the other world to make sure they realize that the way they use their material goods and assets in this life will have eternal consequences in the next. The first comes in Luke 12:13–21 and is known as the parable of the Rich Fool. This man was so successful in his farming that he found himself with far more goods than he could possibly use or enjoy. Therefore he had to decide what he was going to do with them, and in particular where he was going to store them: 'What shall I do', he asked himself, 'for I have nowhere to store my crops?' (12:17).

His answer to this storage problem was short-sighted and foolish in the extreme, even from the limited viewpoint of his own self-inter-est. In the first place he might have observed what our Lord urges us all to notice, that when it comes to goods it is not in the excess of them that our life consists (12:15). A man may enjoy driving a Rolls-Royce car, but he can't enjoy driving five all at the same time.

Secondly, he might have observed how uncertain the length of one's life is. To 'have ample goods laid up for many years' (12:19) may be all right if you can be sure that you are going to have many years on earth in which to enjoy them. But if you have stored up massive amounts of excess goods on earth and then your life on earth is suddenly terminated, you not only do not have the opportunity to enjoy the goods on earth, but you cannot take them with you, and so you lose the lot.

That is very poor business policy and well merits the rebuke which the voice administered to the rich fool: 'This night your soul is required of you, and the things you have prepared, whose will they be?' (12:20). It would make much more sense to take the excess of material goods that you do not need and you cannot enjoy, and translate them into spiritual capital, which can be transferred to the other world, so that you arrive there not only saved but with a good spiritual foundation and potential for enjoying eternity.

'Lay up for yourselves treasures in heaven,' said our Lord (Matt 6:20); and if we ask how it is done, the short answer is the one Paul gives in 1 Timothy:

> As for the rich in this present age, charge them not to be haughty, nor to set their hopes on the uncertainty of riches, but on God, who richly provides us with everything to enjoy. They are to do good, to be rich in good works, to be generous and ready to share, thus storing up treasure for themselves as a good foundation for the future, so that they may take hold of that which is truly life. (1 Tim 6:17-19)

Future treasure

The other parable is to be found in Luke 16:1–13, and it is known as the parable of the Unjust Steward. It describes a steward who was dismissed from his position. There was a short interval between being given notice and actually leaving his job, and he decided that, while he still had his employer's goods in his hands, he would be wise to use those goods in such a way that, when eventually he had to give them up, he would have friends in the world outside who would be kind to him and give him a home.

The way he set about doing this was in fact quite unscrupulous, but that is beside the point. The point is that he looked ahead and used his present stewardship to make friends for the future. In that, said our Lord, he was wiser than some Christians. All of us have assets of one kind or another, which incidentally our Lord calls 'unrighteous wealth', presumably because here on earth assets and income are unequally, and often unfairly, distributed. Be that as it may, we are to use these assets, he said, in such a way that, when they are done and gone forever and we have to pass over into eternity, we may have friends in eternity who will receive us into their eternal habitations.

Notice, of course, that our Lord did not tell us to use our assets to obtain salvation for ourselves, which would be an impossibility because salvation cannot be earned or bought. It is a gift given altogether *ex gratia* to the undeserving who are prepared to repent and believe. But having friends is a different matter: we are to use our assets to make friends.

Now, the idea that in heaven some people will have friends and others will not, comes to some people as a shock, and they find it difficult to understand. So let us take a realistic example. Picture an older Christian widow whose meagre weekly income is barely sufficient to cover her needs. By means of self-denial and careful stewardship she finds that at the end of one week she has a pound to spare, and out of love for the Lord and her fellow men she decides to spend the pound on paying for Gospels to be sent to tribespeople in the rainforests of Peru. Through reading these Gospels eventually fifty of them come to faith in Christ. When at last it is revealed at the judgment seat of Christ that it was this woman's pound that was the means of bringing them the gospel, will they not feel a special and eternal gratitude towards her?

By way of contrast, now suppose there is another Christian, this time a man. He has a town house, three country estates, a fleet of cars, an ocean-going yacht and a few other items. He too finds that at the end of the week he has a pound left over from his weekly income, and he decides to spend it on ice cream. Now, there is nothing sinful about ice cream, so far as is known; but when at the judgment seat of

Christ it comes out that that is how the man spent his spare pound, it is unlikely that any tribespeople or anyone else will feel any surge of gratitude or friendship towards him on that account.

Of course, in God's heaven everybody is loved; but to have no friends who have reason to feel special gratitude and friendship towards you is to suffer an eternal loss. If we were wise, we should contrive to devote more than a pound a week to the making of friends for eternity. More in fact than just money; it would not be extravagance to use everything that God has entrusted to our stewardship primarily to that end.

The Gospel of the King and his Present Kingdom

The King Announces his Covenant

Now the Feast of Unleavened Bread drew near, which is called the Passover. And the chief priests and the scribes were seeking how to put him to death, for they feared the people.

Then Satan entered into Judas called Iscariot, who was of the number of the twelve. He went away and conferred with the chief priests and officers how he might betray him to them. And they were glad, and agreed to give him money. So he consented and sought an opportunity to betray him to them in the absence of a crowd.

Then came the day of Unleavened Bread, on which the Passover lamb had to be sacrificed. So Jesus sent Peter and John, saying, 'Go and prepare the Passover for us, that we may eat it.'

They said to him, 'Where would you have us prepare it?' He said to them, 'Behold, when you have entered the city, a man carrying a jar of water will meet you. Follow him into the house that he enters and tell the master of the house, "The Teacher says to you, Where is the guest room, where I may eat the Passover with my disciples?" And he will show you a large upper room furnished; prepare it there.'

And they went and found it just as he had told them, and they prepared the Passover.

And when the hour came, he reclined at table, and the apostles with him. And he said to them, 'I have earnestly desired to eat this Passover with you before I suffer. For I tell you I will not eat it until it is fulfilled in the kingdom of God.'

And he took a cup, and when he had given thanks he said, 'Take this, and divide it among yourselves. For I tell you that from now on I will not drink of the fruit of the vine until the kingdom of God comes.'

And he took bread, and when he had given thanks, he broke it and gave it to them, saying, 'This is my body, which is given for you. Do this in remembrance of me.'

And likewise the cup after they had eaten, saying, 'This cup that is poured out for you is the new covenant in my blood.'

Luke 22:1–20

No one now knows the name of the man who let our Lord have the use of a room in his house for the celebration of the Last Supper; but whoever he was, he did a very brave thing. Jerusalem at that time was hostile to Christ. Its rulers had determined to crucify him; their only problem was how they could manage to arrest him when the city was so full of pilgrims, many of whom were sympathetic towards Christ and enjoyed listening to him preach. To have attempted to arrest him during the day, when the people thronged him in their hundreds, would have been to invite a riot. Their only hope of doing it, therefore, was either to wait until the Feast was over and all the pilgrims had returned home, or else to do it at night.

During Holy Week, Christ would come into the temple and teach the people during the hours of daylight, but as soon as night fell he would leave the city and disappear into the darkness of the surrounding hills. It would not have been prudent for him to stay in the city after dark. But on the night of the Last Supper, Christ determined to eat the supper with his disciples in the middle of the city in spite of all the hostility that surrounded them. And so it had to be done secretly, and elaborate precautions were taken.

To get the supper ready, two disciples were sent into the city with instructions to look out for a man carrying a pitcher of water. This evidently was some pre-arranged sign. Without saying anything to him, they were to follow him, notice the house he went into, and presently enter the house themselves and ask for the owner. When he appeared, they were simply to say, 'The Teacher says to you, Where is the guest room, where I may eat the Passover with my disciples?' (Luke 22:11). At this, the man would show them a large upper room and they were to prepare the meal there.

When all was ready and night had fallen, Christ unobtrusively entered the city and gathered his disciples round him in this borrowed upper room. For a few brief hours the upper room, cosy and comfortable in the mellow light of its oil lamps, gave them shelter from the hostility that breathed in the darkness outside. But not from all hostility, nor even from the worst; for Satan, who had dogged the path of Christ throughout his earthly ministry, now began to take up position for the final assault. For months past he had worked on the love of money that enslaved the heart of Judas Iscariot, one of Christ's twelve disciples, until Judas no longer had any power or desire to resist evil; and now at this opportune moment he began to press home his advantage. He first put it into his heart to betray the Saviour (compare Luke 22:3 with John 13:2), and before the supper was ended he demanded personal entry into Judas to commandeer and rule him completely.

Consider, then, the situation. A few days earlier, Christ had ridden into the city formally claiming to be her king, and he had been acclaimed by the multitudes. But the city of the great king was now in the hands of rebel forces; and even one of the disciples had sold himself to the archenemy. Yet that night in the face of implacable hatred and in the teeth of satanic opposition, the king set up his kingdom and instituted the covenant that should define the relations between himself as sovereign and his subjects.

Two classes of men

Contrast these two men: the unnamed man, who opened his house to the Saviour for him to turn it into a throne room and set up his kingdom in the midst of the world's opposition; and Judas Iscariot, who was determined to get rid of Christ and found it involved opening his heart to Satan's occupation.

In a sense they represent the only alternatives open to anyone. The idea that we by ourselves are completely free is an illusion. Already sin has made us something less than kings in our own castles. The only way to secure real and permanent freedom is to open the innermost control room of our lives to Christ and allow him to establish himself there as sovereign. But too often we fight for our imagined independence, unaware that the very suggestion to resist the advance of our Creator comes from a more sinister mind than our own. Let Judas remind us that determination to get rid of Christ weakens a person's moral defences to the point where complete takeover by Satan is eventually irresistible.

But suppose a person opens their heart and life without reserve to Christ, for him to rule there as absolute monarch, what kind of a king will Christ prove to be and what will be the nature of his government? To answer these questions, we must look further at what happened on that historic night in the secrecy of the upper room.

The first major thing to happen was that Christ took bread and gave it to his disciples to eat, saying, "This is my body, which is given for you. Do this in remembrance of me." And likewise the cup after they had eaten, saying, "This cup that is poured out for you is the new covenant in my blood.'" (Luke 22:19–20).

Notice that he did not say, this is a new covenant, but the new covenant: that is, he was referring to a particular and well known new covenant, namely, the one that the prophet Jeremiah had foretold (Jer 31:31–34). Notice again that he described it as the new covenant, that is, to contrast it with the old covenant that God had made with Israel after the Exodus on the basis of the law of Moses.

The old covenant

What, then, is meant by a covenant in this spiritual context? We can illustrate the matter by the customs prevalent in the world in the days of Moses. In those times great emperors would draw up treaties with their vassal kings, which would remind these subject kings just who the great emperor was, what benefits he had conferred on them, what behaviour was expected from the vassals, what blessings would accrue to them if they obeyed the emperor, and what punishments they would incur if they rebelled against him. In other words, these treaties spelled out the relationship between the great sovereign and his subjects.

These treaties were called covenants, and the old covenant was, so to speak, a treaty between God and the Israelites, which defined the relationship between him as their sovereign and them as his subjects. Its preamble (Exod 20:2) reminds the Israelites who the divine emperor is: 'I am the LORD your God', and proceeds to rehearse what he has done for them: 'who brought you out of the land of Egypt, out of the house of slavery.' (Incidentally this very preamble shows that Gentiles were never put under this covenant, though many people, Christians included, have imagined they were: God never at any time brought us Gentiles out of the land of Egypt.)

In the ten major commandments and scores of lesser ones, the covenant then goes on to specify the conduct required by God in the Israelites. It makes provision for the covenant documents to be stored in the ark (Exod 25:21), and for the terms of the covenant to be read publicly before the assembled nation once in every seven years. Then it details the curses that would come upon them if they were disobedient, and the blessings that would follow their right behaviour (Deut 31:10–13; 11:26–28; 27:11–28:68).

It is clear that the old covenant, although based on God's moral law, was much more than moral instruction and advice. It spelled out the terms upon which God was prepared to enter into relationship with Israel and be their God. He was prepared to receive them and to bless them, to acknowledge them as his people, so long as they kept all the requirements of his moral law; but if they broke that law or for any reason failed to keep it, then it warned them that God would curse and reject them.

The difference between the law as moral instruction and the law as the basis of a covenant relationship is exceedingly important. Let's use a simple illustration to help ourselves grasp it. Think of one of the famous cookbooks you know, one of the world famous collections of exceedingly good and well-proven recipes. If a person carried out its instructions fully, he or she would be an incredibly good cook. Now it is perhaps just conceivable that a young man, upon getting married, might present his new wife with such a cookbook as something more than a hint of the standards of cooking he would like her to aim at; and it is perhaps conceivable that, if she were a sweet-tempered young woman, she might accept the book with a smile, if not with enthusiasm. But suppose the young man were to explain that in offering her this cookbook he was laying down the basis of their relationship. As long as she faithfully carried out to the letter all the instructions in the book perfectly and without failure, he would be willing to accept her as his wife, nourish, love and cherish her. But if she failed to perform the instructions perfectly, if ever she burned the soup, undercooked the meat or spoiled the lemon meringue, he would be obliged to repudiate and divorce her. I suspect there would not be a woman on earth willing to become his wife on those terms.

Yet something like this, only infinitely more exacting, was the covenant Israel entered into with God. His law, to sum it up, said they were to love the Lord their God with all their heart, mind, soul and strength, and their neighbour as themselves. So long as they did so without failure or deviation, God was prepared to be their God, to accept them and to bless them. But if, through weakness or waywardness, they failed to keep his law, in part or whole, then with their consent he was to repudiate and curse them.

It is altogether remarkable that Israel ever consented to such a covenant. That they readily did so certainly shows how zealous and religious they were, but also how little they knew the weakness and sinfulness of their own hearts. Moses scarcely had time to bring the tables of the law down from the mountain to the people before they had broken the most fundamental of all its requirements.

Yet in spite of Israel's failure, repeated over many long centuries, to keep her part of the covenant, and in spite of the sorrow and divine chastisement she has brought upon herself thereby, one can still find people even in Christendom who imagine that a true and satisfactory relationship with God can be built on those same terms of keeping the old covenant. They may not express their idea in such theological terms as we have just used. They tend to say something more like this: 'Well, I believe that if I do my best to keep the commandments, to serve God and love my neighbour, everything will turn out all right for me in the end.' But of course it won't. It couldn't. What they call doing their best to keep the commandments, turns out, when you examine it, not to be a keeping of them but a failure to keep them: a twenty-five percent failure, more or less, but always a failure to keep them perfectly. And if they insist on a relationship with God that depends on their faulty efforts to keep his law, then God will have no option but to reject them as he rejected Israel.

A two-party covenant

This whole attitude is centuries out of date. The Jewish prophet Jeremiah in the sixth century BC had already seen that it was impossible for humanity to have a satisfactory relationship with God on the terms of the old covenant, and he was inspired by God to prophesy that one day God would make a new covenant on different terms. When, therefore, in the upper room in Jerusalem our Lord handed his disciples a cup of wine and said, 'This cup . . . is the new covenant in my blood' (Luke 22:20), his disciples would know that he was announcing the inauguration of the new covenant that Jeremiah had described. It was to revolutionize mankind's relationship with God.

But then, in what sense is the new covenant new and different from the old? It is new in two respects: in its basic nature and in its terms. In its basic nature the new covenant is a one-party covenant, whereas the old covenant was a two-party covenant. Let us illustrate the difference by a simple analogy. Suppose you want a new house, and you engage

Mr Smith to build you one. It is more than likely that you will draw up an agreement, or covenant, with Mr Smith. The covenant will of course be a two-party covenant in which both you and the builder have some conditions to fulfil. It is written into the agreement that he is to build you a two storey, four bedroom, family home, and that upon the completion of this house according to all the detailed specifications, you for your part are required to pay him £200,000. It is also written into the covenant that if either party should fail to fulfil any or all of the conditions laid down, the appropriate penalties will be exacted.

Now the old covenant was a two-party covenant like that. God had his part to fulfil: he was to accept Israel as his people and to bless them abundantly. But it depended on Israel fulfilling their conditions, which were to keep all God's law perfectly. And it was written into the covenant that if Israel failed to keep their side, the penalty would be God's curse upon them.

Israel did fail: 'they did not abide by the terms of that covenant, and I abandoned them, says the Lord' (Heb 8:9 NEB). And so, says God in this same passage, the old covenant has to be put aside and a new and different one introduced:

> Behold, the days are coming, declares the Lord, when I will make a new covenant with the house of Israel and the house of Judah, not like the covenant that I made with their fathers on the day when I took them by the hand to bring them out of the land of Egypt, my covenant that they broke . . . (Jer 31:31–32)

The fault was not in the standards required by that old covenant; nor is God nowadays proposing to content himself with a much more permissive and tolerant law than in Old Testament days. The fault was with sinful mankind's inability to keep the terms of any two-party covenant between themselves and God, based on God's law.

The new one-party covenant

So let us consider now that other type of covenant that we have called a one-party covenant. Suppose one day you get a letter from the local solicitors, Cunningham and Craft, informing you that your great uncle John has just died in America. You never knew Uncle John: he emigrated to America before you were born, and never came back. You are as sorry as you can manage to be to hear he has died, but at the same time overwhelmed with unexpected delight to learn that he has left you his accumulated fortune of a million dollars. You hurry to the solicitors and ask what conditions you have to fulfil in order to get your hands on the dollars. They learnedly read the clauses of the will and announce that you have no conditions to fulfil beyond being prepared to receive the money. You retort that you don't deserve it! You never did anything for Uncle John while he was alive; surely you'll have to do something meritorious now before you receive such large benefits.

The solicitors re-read the will and affirm that in all its clauses there is nothing required of you except the willingness to receive this undeserved gift. You then ask how you can be sure that the money is yours and no one will be able to prevent it coming to you. They reply that Uncle John has not only given you the money but he has made a covenant, a one-party covenant. In other words, he has made a will, which, though it lays down no conditions for you to fulfil, binds his executors to give you the money and forbids anyone else running off with it. Of course, if you want to, you can refuse to accept the money. You can tear up the will, laugh at the solicitors for believing it, and go home. But if you want to benefit from John's will you merely have to believe and receive it, because the will is a one-party covenant.

The new covenant is a one-party covenant like that (see Gal 3:15–22). It is what in modern parlance we call a will, or testament, to distinguish it from two-party covenants; which is why we call the twenty-seven books that detail all its benefits and provisions the New Testament. The blessings and benefits that the new covenant confers on those who believe and receive the Saviour are immense, but they are all guaranteed to the believer because Christ himself is the guarantor (Heb 7:22).

Of course, all are free to reject or neglect those blessings if they want to, and many do. Someone may even go further and deny that the New Testament is worth the paper it is written on. No one will force us to accept the blessings of the new covenant against our will. God's grace is infinite but not irresistible. But if we would receive and enjoy the benefits of the new covenant, we can and must dismiss all thought of deserving them, and accept them freely by faith from the hand of him who offered us the cup of his covenant and signed the covenant itself, so to speak, with his own blood.

The Relationship *between the* Sovereign *and his* Subjects

And likewise the cup after they had eaten, saying, 'This cup that is poured out for you is the new covenant in my blood.'

Luke 22:20

But as it is, Christ has obtained a ministry that is as much more excellent than the old as the covenant he mediates is better, since it is enacted on better promises. For if that first covenant had been faultless, there would have been no occasion to look for a second. For he finds fault with them when he says:

> 'Behold, the days are coming, declares the Lord, when I will establish a new covenant with the house of Israel and with the house of Judah, not like the covenant that I made with their fathers on the day when I took them by the hand to bring them out of the land of Egypt. For they did not continue in my covenant, and so I showed no concern for them, declares the Lord. For this is the covenant that I will make with the house of Israel after those days, declares the Lord: I will put my laws into their minds, and write them on their hearts, and I will be their God, and they shall be my people. And they shall not teach, each one his neighbour and each one his brother, saying, 'Know the Lord', for they shall all know me, from the least of them to the greatest. For I will be merciful towards their iniquities, and I will remember their sins no more.'

In speaking of a new covenant, he makes the first one obsolete. And what is becoming obsolete and growing old is ready to vanish away.

Hebrews 8:6–13

In our previous chapter we noticed that the new covenant is different from the old in its basic nature: it is a one-party covenant, whereas the old covenant is a two-party agreement. Now we must notice how different and superior the new covenant is in its detailed terms. These terms, which spell out the relationship between the divine king and his believing subjects, are conveniently set out in Hebrews 8:10–12. They fall into three groups. The first group comes in verse 10 where God says 'I will put my laws into their minds, and write them on their hearts.' The point of this promise can be seen, if we remember that the Ten Commandments of the old covenant were written on two tablets of stone. That was the reason why they were so ineffective in getting people to do God's will. They were simply commands written externally on hard, cold stone: they told a person what to do, but they could give them no strength to do it; they told a person what not to do, but they could give them no power to refrain from doing it. They were in themselves perfectly good and reasonable commands, and if a person could have kept them, they would have produced in them a most noble character. But humans cannot keep them. Our hearts are weak and sinful, deceitful above all things, as the Old Testament puts it, and desperately sick (see Jer 17:9).

God's law within

Before anyone could have any hope of keeping God's law in a manner that would satisfy God, they would need to be given a completely new heart, a new nature, a new power. And therefore it is precisely this that the first clause in the new covenant provides for. God's undertaking to write his law on a person's heart means far more than helping that person to remember it so that they could, if necessary, repeat it off by heart. It means nothing less than the implantation within them of a new nature, the very nature of God, in fact (see 2 Pet 1:3–4). For, as Romans 8:7 puts it, 'the mind that is set on the flesh is hostile to God, for it does not submit to God's law; indeed, it cannot'; and therefore, if a person is going to fulfil God's law, God must create within them a new life that by its very nature does the law of God. John the apostle calls the process by which it is done a 'new birth'; the new covenant calls it 'the writing of God's law on our hearts'.

The next clause in the covenant provides that each believer shall enjoy an intimate knowledge of God in his personal experience.

It runs: 'I will be their God, and they shall be my people. And they shall not teach, each one his neighbour and each one his brother, saying, "Know the Lord", for they shall all know me, from the least of them to the greatest' (Heb 8:10–11).

Knowing God

Knowing God in this sense is not just a matter of knowing that there is a God. The verb 'to know' is one that we use of the intimate relationship between a man and his wife. At the spiritual level knowing God denotes a personal, direct, intimate relationship with God. Second-hand experience of God conveyed through books, or preachers or priests may have a real and positive value. But it is not enough.

However much other people may help us to understand things about God, in order to experience salvation, to have God's law written on our hearts, we must know God personally and directly ourselves. A woman may first come to know of her husband-to-be through the glowing reports of some friend, and the friend may after a while arrange an introduction. But if ever she is to become the man's wife, there must come a point when the friend gets out of the way and the woman enters a direct and personal relationship with the man.

Moreover, failure to enter such a personal relationship with God is spiritually fatal. Our Lord has himself warned us that when at last he rises up and closes the door, and has to bid those on the outside to depart from him, the reason why they will have to depart will be given in these words: 'I never knew you' (Matt 7:23). That cannot mean Christ never knew they existed, or never knew who they were; it means that they and Christ never had any direct and personal dealings with each other. And Christ further warns us that the fact that these people will be able to cite evidence of having been religious, even above average, will not prove an adequate substitute for personal knowledge of the Saviour (Matt 7:22; Luke 13:26).

Conversely, of the true believer Christ says: 'I am the good shepherd. I know my own and my own know me, just as the Father knows me and I know the Father'; and again, 'My sheep hear my voice, and I know them, and they follow me. I give them eternal life, and they will never perish, and no one will snatch them out of my hand' (John 10:14–15, 27–28).

Now the glorious thing about this personal knowledge of, and relationship with, God is that it is not something that we have to work up and qualify for by means of long and rigorous preparatory disciplines. The new covenant offers it as a gift. It is effected by the Holy Spirit in the heart of everyone who trusts Christ. Listen to Paul: 'And because you are sons, God has sent the Spirit of his Son into our hearts, crying, "Abba! Father!"' (Gal 4:6). When we first trust Christ and become children of God, we are doubtless still very immature, spiritually speaking. We are not yet spiritual fathers, nor even full-grown, strong young men; we are nothing but spiritual little children. Yet John says of such: 'I write to you, children, because you know the Father' (1 John 2:13).

God forgives

The third and final clause in the new covenant runs as follows: 'For I will be merciful toward their iniquities, and I will remember their sins no more' (Heb 8:12). The first stupendous thing about this magnificent clause is that here we have forgiveness of sins written into the terms of the covenant.

To help ourselves see what this means, let us revert for a moment to the illustration we used in a previous study. You want a builder to build you a house. He agrees to do so, but says that it will of course all depend on your paying him the price, £200,000. So you enter a covenant: he is to build the house and you are to pay the £200,000. Suppose, however, when the house is built, you find your business has gone downhill and you cannot pay the required price; it would be an extraordinary thing, verging on the miraculous, if the builder forgave you your debt to which you were bound by the covenant, and let you have the house for nothing. But if that would be extraordinary, it would be altogether unheard of that, from the very beginning, the builder should draw up the contract to say that your having the house depended on you paying the price, but nevertheless if you couldn't pay it he would forgive you and you could have the house without paying for it. Such a statement would be nonsense: a covenant cannot make obtaining the house depend both on paying the price and not paying it.

Similarly, no divine covenant could make salvation depend both on keeping the law and not keeping it. The old covenant made it dependent on keeping the law and pronounced God's curse on those who did not keep it. The new covenant, far from making salvation depend on keeping the law, writes into its terms guaranteed forgiveness for failure to keep it. God could not now refuse that forgiveness without breaking the covenant, which of course he has no intention of doing. All who trust Christ therefore can be absolutely certain of forgiveness with a certainty based on the unbreakable faithfulness of God in keeping any covenant he makes.

But at this point someone is sure to object that if the covenant guarantees forgiveness so that we can be sure of it in advance, it would be nothing better than the old medieval scandal in which you could buy indulgences in advance for sins you had not yet done but intended doing. So you could proceed to commit the sins with the certainty of being forgiven, and therefore with virtual impunity.

The answer to the objection is that it forgets what the first clause of the new covenant says. That clause expresses God's determination to write his laws on the heart of the believer, so that, as Paul would put it, 'the righteous requirement of the law might be fulfilled in us, who walk not according to the flesh but according to the Spirit' (Rom 8:4). That is, the new covenant does not simply provide forgiveness; rather, the very first clause announces that its prime objective is to make a person holy by the progressive work of the Holy Spirit in the person's heart and guarantees that God will not give up until he has made them perfect.

Only in this context does the third clause assure believers that God's acceptance of us does not depend on our spiritual progress, and certainly not on our attaining to perfection. In the school of progressive holiness we will have many difficult lessons to face, and our mistakes and failures will be numerous. But we may find courage and comfort in God's guarantee of complete forgiveness, in the knowledge that we can never lose our acceptance with God and that the goal of perfection will at last be attained.

God forgets

Now let's consider the extensiveness of the forgiveness provided here. To start with, the promise 'I will remember their sins no more' does not mean that God will try to forget the fact that they have sinned.

'Remember' is a legal term. It means 'to remember and take the due legal action about.' When Revelation 18:5 says of Babylon, 'her sins are heaped high as heaven, and God has remembered her iniquities', there follows a description of the judgments that fall on her as God reviews her sins and passes judgment on them. Clause 3 of the covenant, therefore, is saying that God will never bring up believers' sins against them in the legal sense, and will never execute upon them the penalty that those sins deserve.

This is not because God has grown sentimental about the sins of believers or because he treats them as favourites whose sins are to be indulged. It is because Christ has himself paid the penalty. That is why, when he instituted the covenant, he handed to his disciples a cup, the wine in which symbolized 'my blood of the [new] covenant, which is poured out for many for the forgiveness of sins' (Matt 26:28).

God's forgiveness is never anything less than just. Take for example people like King David, Isaiah and Jeremiah who lived under the terms of the old covenant. Like the rest of us, they were sinners and therefore incurred the penalties of that old covenant. How then could they be forgiven and saved? Someone will say, 'But why could they not be transferred, so to speak, from the old covenant and given the benefits of the new?' The answer is, they could. Indeed, according to Hebrews 9:15 that is precisely what God has done for them. But he has not done it by deciding to break the old covenant himself, dishonour its terms, and disregard the very sanctions to which he had pledged himself.

God is not like Adolf Hitler who, when it suited him, was in the habit of solemnly concluding treaties and covenants with other nations; and then, when it ceased to suit him, tore them up and conveniently forgot all about them. Before God could transfer people from their obligation to the old covenant and introduce them to the benefits of the new, all the debts that they had contracted under the old covenant had to be paid. And so says Hebrews 9:15, 'a death' [i.e. the death of Christ] took place 'that redeems them from the transgressions committed under the first covenant', that those 'who are called may receive the promised eternal inheritance.'

Someone will perhaps object that all this makes God appear to be legalistic and exacting, whereas he is kind and loving. But the objection springs from a sentimental and inadequate view of what true love is. Would it be love in the Almighty to bind himself solemnly by a covenant one day to do various things and then forget or refuse to do them the next? We have all come across the parent who is forever promising her spoilt child that if he does such and such a thing again she will punish him; and yet, when the child repeatedly does such and such a thing she lets him off without punishment. That child does not grow up to admire his mother for being loving; he early learns to hold both her word and mother herself in contempt.

If God failed to fulfil the sanctions of his law to which he solemnly committed himself, how could anyone ever be sure he would not like-wise fail to fulfil the promises made to benefit and bless the believer? No, as surely as God bound himself by the terms of the old covenant to enforce the sanctions of his law against sin, so surely were those sanctions enforced when Christ offered himself as a sacrifice for sin. By that same token, as surely as God has bound himself by the terms of the new covenant never to remember believers' sins against them, so surely may they be confident that they will not come into judgment, and that 'there is therefore now no condemnation for those who are in Christ Jesus' (Rom 8:1).

The complete sacrifice

The completeness of the forgiveness offered under the terms of the new covenant can be seen from yet another consideration, namely the fact that Christ's sacrifice is finished and never needs to be repeated. It is common knowledge, of course, that having offered himself as a sacrifice for sin on the cross, Christ has now ascended to heaven and sits at the right hand of God.

No priest ever sat while offering a sacrifice; the only proper pos-ture to adopt in the act of sacrifice was to stand. As Hebrews 10:11 says of the ancient Jewish priests: 'And every priest stands daily at his service, offering repeatedly the same sacrifices, which can never take away sins.' But Christ is not now standing; he is sitting. And the reason is that he is no longer offering any sacrifice for sins. All the work of sacrifice is finished, and Christ has retired from that work altogether. As verse twelve puts it, 'But when Christ had offered for all time a single sacrifice for sins, he sat down at the right hand of God.'

So the question naturally arises: Why is there no need for Christ to continue offering himself as a sacrifice? Why does he not still have to suffer the legal sanctions against sin whenever a believer sins? The Holy Spirit himself gives the answer to this question (10:17–18). He points to the third clause in the new covenant, 'I will remember their sins and their lawless deeds no more.' He then asks us to make the simple and obvious deduction: if all sins are completely forgiven, there is no need for the process of sacrifice to continue, 'where there is forgiveness of these, there is no longer any offering for sin.'

One final point about the third clause of the new covenant. It begins with the little word 'for': 'For I will be merciful towards their iniquities, and I will remember their sins no more' (8:12). This shows that the third clause is meant to explain how the promises of the previous clause can be put into effect. That clause promised that every believer would enjoy an intimate knowledge of God based on a direct and personal relationship with him. But how could anyone enjoy a personal and direct relationship with God, if they had to live in constant uncertainty whether God would eventually accept or reject them?

We all know the lasting psychological damage that children can suffer if in their formative years they are uncertain of acceptance by their parents and live in fear, conscious or subconscious, that one day their parents might reject them. And yet there are multitudes even of religious folk whose relationship with God is haunted by that basic fear and uncertainty, so much so that the very idea of claiming to be sure of salvation strikes them as alarming presumption. And yet it is God's wish to cast out that fear. As John puts it: 'There is no fear in love, but perfect love casts out fear. For fear has to do with punishment, and whoever fears has not been perfected in love' (1 John 4:18). Therefore, in order that the promise of clause 2 of the covenant should be realized and the believer enjoy a secure relationship with God, clause 3 provides the guarantee of complete and utter forgiveness. And it does so, not merely in order that the believer should feel secure and be free from the servility of fear, but because perfect security of relationship with God is the only adequate basis from which the holiness of character that clause 1 guarantees could be developed.

The Rank *and* Reward *of the* King's Servants

A dispute also arose among them, as to which of them was to be regarded as the greatest. And he said to them, 'The kings of the Gentiles exercise lordship over them, and those in authority over them are called benefactors. But not so with you. Rather, let the greatest among you become as the youngest, and the leader as one who serves. For who is the greater, one who reclines at table or one who serves? Is it not the one who reclines at table? But I am among you as the one who serves.

'You are those who have stayed with me in my trials, and I assign to you, as my Father assigned to me, a kingdom, that you may eat and drink at my table in my kingdom and sit on thrones judging the twelve tribes of Israel.'

Luke 22:24–30

In the previous two chapters we concentrated on the new covenant in which is set out the relationship between the king and his subjects. Some people react quite strongly against the whole idea that Christ's relationship with his people should be expressed in terms of a covenant. They say it makes it sound far too severe and legal, when legality is the last thing that should enter into truly personal relationships. And further, when Christ is described as a king and his people as subjects, their resentment boils over into opposition.

Their reaction springs from one of two sources, or perhaps a mixture of both. One source is the modern idea that all assertion of authority is by definition a bad thing, and all submission to authority a mark of servility. People of this persuasion would have everyone equal, with no one possessing or exercising any authority over anyone else. They do not normally campaign, it is true, for the abolition of the force of gravity on the grounds that the sun exercises a greater gravitational pull over the earth than the earth does over the sun. But the physical chaos they would cause if they could switch off gravity, would be no greater than the moral chaos that would result if they could abolish all authority in human relationships, let alone between humanity and God. A mother who declined to exercise any authority over her two-year-old child would cease to be a mother; she would probably find herself prosecuted on grounds of gross neglect. Should her baby grab a bottle of poison and go to drink it, she must exercise fast and firm authority. Love and instinct both demand it.

Everybody equal?

Willingness and courage to face the facts are the sign of maturity. If a schoolboy has worked out his sum under the false impression that the square root of 49 is 24, the teacher who is afraid to tell him that he is wrong—in case the authority of the facts should upset his ego and induce in him an inferiority complex—is helping the boy to remain in the unreal dream world of an infant, thus arresting the process of his growing up.

Will anyone seriously maintain that the drug dealer's views on drug-taking have equal authority with those of the neurologist and the nurses in the hospital for nervous and mental diseases?

Certainly, if the captain of a liner is not allowed to issue peremptory orders to the engineers and the deckhands, but all must be given an equal say in how the ship should be manoeuvred, I pray that I shall never be on board their liner during a storm.

There can be no yielding here to sentimental egalitarianism. Life without authority would be chaos, even if it survived. And a Christ who neither possessed nor asserted authority would be no Saviour of the world but altogether bogus. It is in fact a mark of the genuineness of Christ's claim to be the Son of God, that, while he was meek and lowly in heart, and ever compassionate and merciful, he nevertheless claimed paramount and absolute authority.

The abuse of authority

But the hostile reaction to authority may spring from bitter experience of some abuse of authority; some tyranny in the home, the state or the church. And of all tyrannies, that which is exercised in the name of Christ and the church is of course the worst. In a sense, I suppose, we should not be surprised whenever we come across it, for our Lord himself warned us before he left that such abuses would occur in his kingdom, and he told us what he would eventually do with them. Listen to this passage:

> But if that servant says to himself, 'My master is delayed in coming', and begins to beat the male and female servants, and to eat and drink and get drunk, the master of that servant will come on a day when he does not expect him and at an hour he does not know, and will cut him in pieces and put him with the unfaithful. (Luke 12:45–46)

These are very severe words, but designedly so. All three synoptic Gospels make it clear that nothing angered our Lord so much as the sight of people being oppressed by religious leaders abusing their authority. And he took no pains to conceal his anger. Listen to him preaching in Jerusalem:

> And in the hearing of all the people he said to his disciples, 'Beware of the scribes, who like to walk around in long robes, and love greetings in the market-places and the best seats in the synagogues and the places of honour at feasts, who devour widows' houses

and for a pretence make long prayers. They will receive the greater condemnation.' (20:45–47)

And so it was that when an argument broke out among the apostles at the Last Supper, our Lord took the occasion to teach them what is the true nature of rule and office and service in his kingdom. The argument on that solemn and most sacred occasion had been about which of them was to be regarded as greatest. That one apostle should desire to be regarded as greater than another apostle would surely strike us as incredible, did we not know our own hearts and recognize that the apostles, for all the importance of their office, were human like ourselves. But so it was, and our Lord had to point out to them how thoroughly unregenerate an idea of power and ruling they had imbibed without thinking: 'The kings of the Gentiles exercise lordship over them, and those in authority over them are called benefactors' (22:25).

And still today all too often greatness is felt to lie not in actually serving other people but in the personal aggrandizement that accompanies high office, and in the sense of power and the ability to control other people's lives that high position brings. By some curious twist in logic, the title of Benefactor doesn't go to the people who actually do the work and serve, but to those who sit aloft and are served by others. 'But not so among you', said our Lord to his apostles. They might be destined to hold high office in the church, so high that none could be higher save Christ himself; but they were not to get it into their heads that office in the church was like office in the great pagan empires. 'But not so with you,' said Christ. 'Rather, let the greatest among you become as the youngest, and the leader as one who serves' (22:26).

A perfect example

Now it is evident that a government whose officials behaved themselves in this way would be the beginning of heaven on earth. But Christ's teaching was not just idealistic, unreal, empty talk. What he preached to his apostles, he had already done himself and was still doing. 'For who is the greater,' he said, 'one who reclines at table or one who serves? Is it not the one who reclines at table? But I am among you as the one who serves' (22:27).

How true that was! Luke tells us (18:35–43) that once when Christ was approaching the town of Jericho, a blind beggar sitting by the roadside heard the commotion of the approaching crowd, and discovering that it was Jesus coming, surrounded by a vast throng of people, decided to appeal to Christ to do something about his blindness. Being very tactful—or was it that for all his blindness he had a good deal more insight than most?—he hailed Christ as the Son of David, that is, as the great and glorious king of Israel, and pleaded with him to have mercy on him.

The crowd told him to shut up. 'Look,' they doubtless said, 'there's no use your shouting like that. Jesus is a very important person. In fact, it's quite possible that, like you say, he is the great king himself; and if not that, he is certainly a tremendous preacher and prophet. Kings and prophets can't keep stopping at every corner to see to the needs of flea-bitten beggars. Jesus has more important things to see to.' But at that moment Christ came up level with the blind beggar, and stopped. 'Help that man up and bring him to me', he said to some of the bystanders. And then as the man came near, he asked him, 'Did you call me? Did you want something?' 'Yes,' faltered the man, 'my eyes . . . I'm blind, you know. Could you, I mean, would you give me sight?' 'Why, of course,' said Christ, 'that's why I've come, to serve people.' And immediately he gave the man sight.

That was dramatic, and doubtless it was meant to be. Not in order to make a good showing and get a good write-up in the press, but that all might know that Christ's idea of what it means to be great, to be king, is to serve even the lowest. And we may be sure, now that he has left our lowly world and sits enthroned in glory, that his ideas on being great are the same as they were then. Any one of us in need may kneel and pray, and Christ will still come toward us and say, 'Did you call? Did you want something?' Happy are the subjects who have a king like that!

The lesson in the upper room made an indelible mark on Peter. Listen to him later exhorting the elders of some Christian churches: 'So I exhort the elders among you . . . shepherd the flock of God that is among you . . . not under compulsion, but willingly, as God would have you; not for shameful gain, but eagerly; not domineering over those in your charge, but being examples to the flock' (1 Pet 5:1–3).

And listen, too, to Paul telling the elders in the church of Ephesus the kind of service that is expected of them:

I coveted no one's silver or gold or apparel. You yourselves know that these hands ministered to my necessities and to those who were with me. In all things I have shown you that by working hard in this way we must help the weak and remember the words of the Lord Jesus, how he himself said, 'It is more blessed to give than to receive.' (Acts 20:33–35)

And if this is the attitude and service that is expected of apostles and elders in the church, the lesson for the rest of us is obvious enough.

Rewards

However blessed life under the rule of such a king is, there is no hiding the fact that in the present state of the world, the members of Christ's kingdom will sooner or later find themselves called on to face suffering. But to all who suffer for his sake, Christ holds out the prospect of reward. And so to the apostles in the upper room he went on to say,

You are those who have stayed with me in my trials, and I assign to you, as my Father assigned to me, a kingdom, that you may eat and drink at my table in my kingdom and sit on thrones judging the twelve tribes of Israel. (Luke 22:28–30)

The promised reward contains two elements: the first is a deeper and fuller fellowship with Christ himself—eating and drinking with him at his table; and the second is sharing with him in his reign and practical government. The question arises, when are these rewards to be given? By 'eating and drinking at his table', did our Lord mean partaking in the Lord's Supper in church? And was the phrase, 'sit on thrones judging the twelve tribes of Israel', a picturesque way of saying that the apostles were to have control of the government of the church? Or does the eating and drinking at his table in his kingdom refer to that fuller fellowship with the king that we shall enjoy at his second coming? And does the promise of judging the twelve tribes of Israel mean literally what it says, that in the coming kingdom of Christ, when the church reigns with him, the apostles shall have responsibility for administering the nation of Israel?

The question is by no means merely academic. Early in the history of Christendom, and particularly after the so-called conversion of Constantine, the idea became generally accepted that Christ meant the church to be reigning over the earth now in this age, and therefore it was the responsibility of the church to set up and put down kings. Moreover, it was accompanied by another idea, which suggested that the church was an extension and continuation of the nation of Israel and should therefore behave in the same way.

This had the most unfortunate consequences. For instance, Israel in her better days was a theocracy and her king was regarded as God's immediate viceroy on earth. Religion and politics therefore were virtually one and the same thing, and the religious power was entitled to use the civil power to enforce its rules and regulations. If, for example, the people of a certain town went over to idolatry, they were given due warning; but if they did not repent the king would raise an army, destroy the city and put all its inhabitants to the sword (see Deut 13:12–18).

Therefore, when the church got it into its head that it was meant to be a continuation of Israel, it logically proceeded to behave as though the Church and the State were coterminous, and the civil power was there to enforce the dictates of the church and to punish all who stepped out of line. The persecutions perpetrated by Protestants and Catholics alike on those whom they were pleased to regard as infidels and heretics are grim witness to the thoroughness with which they carried out the idea that the church is the modern Israel meant to be reigning now over the earth.

Future rule

But the whole thing was a ghastly mistake. The reward of reigning with Christ was never meant to be enjoyed now in this age. From the very beginning Christ made it clear that this reward would not be given until his second coming. This is easily seen if we compare the passage before us in Luke with two similar passages in the Gospel of Matthew.

First notice that the phrase, 'sit on thrones, judging the twelve tribes of Israel' occurs virtually word for word in Matthew 19:28:

> Jesus said to them, 'Truly, I say to you, in the new world, when the Son of Man will sit on his glorious throne, you who have followed me will also sit on twelve thrones, judging the twelve tribes of Israel.'

Here the time for judging is said to be when the Son of Man shall sit on the throne of his glory. When is that? We are not left to guess: Matthew tells us explicitly:

> When the Son of Man comes in his glory, and all the angels with him, then he will sit on his glorious throne. Before him will be gathered all the nations, and he will separate people one from another as a shepherd separates the sheep from the goats. (25:31–32)

This is beyond all doubt a description of our Lord's second coming in power and great glory to take over the government of this world and to set up his own kingdom. And this, of course, is how the apostles and the early church understood the matter.

Admittedly some of the Christians at Corinth began to behave as if the time for suffering were past and the time for reigning had come. But Paul administered them a somewhat caustic rebuke:

> Already you have all you want! Already you have become rich! Without us you have become kings! And would that you did reign, so that we might share the rule with you! For ... To the present hour we hunger and thirst, we are poorly dressed and buffeted and homeless, and we labour, working with our own hands. When reviled, we bless; when persecuted, we endure; when slandered, we entreat. We have become, and are still, like the scum of the world, the refuse of all things. (1 Cor 4:8–13)

But if reigning with Christ is not something which is given to Christians now but something promised to them in the future, it is meant to have a profound effect on our life now, inspiring our loyalty and strengthening us to endure our present sufferings for Christ whatever they may be. And, of course, it has had precisely that effect on the martyrs and missionaries and on all who have sacrificed or suffered in any way for Christ's sake and the gospel's.

Let the last word in this connection go once more to Paul. Writing to Timothy from prison, he says:

> Remember Jesus Christ, risen from the dead, the offspring of David, as preached in my gospel, for which I am suffering, bound with chains as a criminal. But the word of God is not bound! Therefore I endure everything for the sake of the elect, that they also may obtain the salvation that is in Christ Jesus with eternal glory. The saying is trustworthy, for:
>
> If we have died with him, we will also live with him;
>   if we endure, we will also reign with him;
> if we deny him, he also will deny us;
>   if we are faithless, he remains faithful—
> for he cannot deny himself. (2 Tim 2:8–13)

The King-Priest *and the* Royal Outlaw

A dispute also arose among them, as to which of them was to be regarded as the greatest. And he said to them, 'The kings of the Gentiles exercise lordship over them, and those in authority over them are called benefactors. But not so with you. Rather, let the greatest among you become as the youngest, and the leader as one who serves. For who is the greater, one who reclines at table or one who serves? Is it not the one who reclines at table? But I am among you as the one who serves. You are those who have stayed with me in my trials, and I assign to you, as my Father assigned to me, a kingdom, that you may eat and drink at my table in my kingdom and sit on thrones judging the twelve tribes of Israel.

Luke 22:24–30

'Simon, Simon, behold, Satan demanded to have you, that he might sift you like wheat, but I have prayed for you that your faith may not fail. And when you have turned again, strengthen your brothers.'

Peter said to him, 'Lord, I am ready to go with you both to prison and to death.'

Jesus said, 'I tell you, Peter, the cock will not crow this day, until you deny three times that you know me.'

And he said to them, 'When I sent you out with no money bag or knapsack or sandals, did you lack anything?'

They said, 'Nothing.'

He said to them, 'But now let the one who has a money bag take it, and likewise a knapsack. And let the one who has no sword sell his cloak and buy one. For I tell you that this Scripture must be fulfilled in me: "And he was numbered with the transgressors." For what is written about me has its fulfilment.'

And they said, 'Look, Lord, here are two swords.'

And he said to them, 'It is enough.'

Luke 22:31–38

The mention of suffering and reward led our Lord next to think of Peter and the storm that had for some while been blowing up and was now about to break over him. Satan was about to make an all-out attack on the little band of apostles, and his special target was to be Simon Peter. Christ foresaw it all; for Satan is not allowed to attack any believer just as he will. Mysterious as God's providential government of the world may appear to our finite understanding, Scripture indicates that before Satan can assault the faith of a believer, he must, so to speak, gain permission.

It was so with Job, the patriarch. Satan is represented as coming before God and complaining that God had placed a hedge round Job that guarded him from all suffering; and that in consequence Job's love for God was little more than a shrewd kind of love that would disappear as soon as Job began to suffer. Satan therefore sought permission to attack Job, confident that if he were allowed to damage his property, family and health, he could eventually bring Job to curse God and so demonstrate that his faith was not true faith after all. Satan was given permission to go ahead and attack; but even then limits were set to what he might do. For, as Paul puts it, 'God is faithful, and he will not let you be tempted beyond your ability, but with the temptation he will also provide the way of escape, that you may be able to endure it' (1 Cor 10:13). God must allow his people's faith to be tested; but he is not prepared to let that faith be broken.

And so when it came to the attack on the apostles, we gather from our Lord's words that Satan had first to seek permission: 'Simon, Simon, behold, Satan demanded to have you, that he might sift you like wheat' (Luke 22:31).

The metaphor is vivid and instructive. One puts wheat through a sieve not to destroy or throw away the good and genuine wheat, but in order to separate the useless chaff from the valuable grain. And whatever may be Satan's motive in attacking believers, the effect of his temptations is to accomplish an end that God himself desires, the removal from a believer's life of all that is light, spurious and worthless, so that what is genuine might stand uncompromised.

Satan's limitations

But whereas Satan was going to attack all twelve apostles, it seems that his main objective was going to be an attempt to destroy Peter's faith beyond any possibility of recovery. Said Christ to Peter, 'But I have prayed for you that your faith may not fail' (22:32). These few words teem with wonderful and beautiful things. First they tell us that Christ not only sees Satan's attacks coming long before the believer who is to be attacked realizes what is happening, but that he also gives himself to prayer to ensure that Satan's foul intentions shall be defeated. With this we encounter what is our Lord's chief present ministry: 'he always lives', says Hebrews 7:25, 'to make intercession for [his people]'.

Notice, however, that his intercessory prayer is not just a vague general intercession for the church as a whole: 'I have prayed for you' (the pronoun is singular), he says to Peter. We are not, of course, to deduce from this that he did not also pray for the others; but we are given to see that our Lord was aware of the special need of each individual and prayed specifically for each man and each need. In ancient Israel, when the high priest entered the presence of God to intercede on the behalf of the people, he wore a breastplate on which were inscribed individually the names of each of the twelve tribes of Israel. But that was only a symbol. The present reality is far more glorious. Every believer may know that as Christ continues his ministry of intercession before God, every name is mentioned individually in the divine presence by an intercessor who knows every individual's personality, weaknesses and peculiar trials.

But notice again what exactly it was that Christ prayed for Peter: he prayed that his faith should not fail. Not that his courage, or his devotion, or his godliness, or his Christian testimony should not fail, but that his faith should not fail. In the event everything else did fail: his nerve went, his courage failed, and his Christian testimony was smashed to smithereens as he stood among the Jewish high priest's servants and used all the swear words he knew to try and convince them that he was not a follower of Christ. But while everything else failed, his faith held fast. Underneath it all he never ceased to be a believer.

The battle of faith

So the battle of faith was won, and it would be impossible to exaggerate how important the victory was. Had it been lost, everything would have been lost. The Bible declares that salvation is a free gift, but it must be received by faith. The terms are: 'whoever believes in the Son has eternal life' (John 3:36). If Satan could smash a believer's faith, the person would no longer be a believer and all would be lost. The relation between God and the one who is saved is a relationship of faith. It has to be: all personal relationships involve faith between the people concerned, and this relationship supremely so—'And without faith it is impossible to please him' (Heb 11:6).

No wonder then that Satan makes it his chief aim to attack and destroy a believer's faith. And it would be a hopeless situation if the believer were at this, the weakest point, left alone to face the fury and subtlety of Satan, uncertain of the outcome. But God, who has provided all the other elements in our salvation, has not overlooked our need at this critical point, but has provided an utterly indestructible defence for our faith in the person of our King–Priest, who 'always lives to make intercession for them' (Heb 7:25).

It goes without saying that all the credit for the survival of Peter's faith belongs to Christ and his intercession; and therefore it is not surprising to learn from Christ's remarks to Peter that the issue was never in doubt. 'When you have turned again,' he said—not if you return, but when you have returned—'strengthen your brothers' (Luke 22:32).

There was no doubt whether he would recover or not. Christ had prayed that his faith should not fail; and Christ has never prayed a prayer that did not secure its objective, and he never will. Granted there were some hours in the courtyard of the high priest when anyone who knew Peter only superficially might well have concluded that he was not a believer; perhaps he had never been a genuine believer at all; or, if he had, his faith must have now disappeared permanently. But in spite of all appearances to the contrary, the underlying fact was that his faith had not, and did not, fail.

And we can be sure that once there has been true and genuine faith exercised in Christ, Christ will maintain that faith. Battered as it may be at times, and compromised as it may appear from the person's outward behaviour, he will maintain it and bring it through to ultimate triumph. And therefore God would have every believer in Christ know and grow strong in the knowledge that 'he is able to save to the uttermost those who draw near to God through him, since he always lives to make intercession for them' (Heb 7:25).

Near failure

Now, when Christ told Peter that he was going to be attacked by Satan, and under the attack he would deny Christ three times over, Peter was understandably upset. He found it so hard to believe, and he felt Christ had judged him unfairly and underestimated the strength of his loyalty and devotion. 'Lord,' he said, 'I am ready to go with you both to prison and to death' (Luke 22:33).

There is no doubt that Peter meant it, and meant it sincerely. He had no lack of physical courage. In Gethsemane, when a squad of soldiers fully armed came up to arrest Christ, Peter drew his sword and went to take them on single-handed. But all unknown to Peter there was a weakness in his makeup; a mixture perhaps of basic nervousness and lack of moral stamina that Satan would know how to play on when he got Peter off his home ground in strange and terrifying circumstances. And so, unable to take Christ's words at their face value and confident as ever in his own natural courage, Peter followed Christ as he was led off by the troops to the high priest's court, and went inside. As Matthew puts it, 'he sat with the guards to see the end' (Matt 26:58). The end of the trial? Who knows, perhaps the end of Christ?

What he saw was not the end of Christ but the end of himself. For presently the sniping began, devilishly accurate and potentially lethal. At once Peter was in trouble; he tried to resist, but it was like trying to resist rifle fire with your bare hands. The questions tore him open, and underneath there was nothing but fear and panic and cowardice. He tried to cover it up; he swore and cursed, but nobody was convinced. They could all see through him. He had never pretended to be brilliant in theology, like John was, but he had always thought of himself as manly and practical; and he loved Christ second to none.

Now his mental picture of himself was shattered, and he was reduced to a gibbering coward by a servant girl and the jeers and threats of a few common soldiers. He couldn't understand it. He felt he was falling into a chasm, and try as frantically as he might to get a handhold somewhere and pull himself up, he could get no grip of himself or anything else. It was nightmarish.

What was that? Oh, only a rooster crowing. Then suddenly he remembered and looked up. In that very moment he saw Christ turn and look straight at him from where he was standing at the other end of the courtyard. Nothing was said, but at once Peter remembered what Christ had said about him in the upper room. And to think he had dared to contradict him! What must Christ think of him now? It was too much; he couldn't face any more. He got up and made for the door. His first instinct must have been to run away; not so much from the high priest's troops, for death at this moment might in some sense have seemed attractive; but to run away from Christ, from his fellow disciples, from his failure and from himself if possible. Rather than come back, it would be easier to abandon all profession of faith and affect a careless cynical attitude.

But in Peter's mind that rooster wouldn't stop crowing. He could hear it crow once and then again, just as Christ had said it would. Each time it crowed he relived the whole thing over again in all its shameful detail. It tormented him.

Presently it was as though a dark cloud was lifting and light was shining through again. 'That was what Christ was trying to say to me as he looked at me from the other end of the room! It was when the rooster crowed the second time and I looked up that he deliberately turned and looked at me. So he wasn't reproaching me; he was wanting to remind me that he had known all about it before it happened. I only then discovered what a failure I was, but he had always known it. He must have known it when he told us, "God did not send his Son into the world to condemn the world, but in order that the world might be saved through him" (John 3:17). When I first came to him, and he said that I was Simon but that he was going to make me into a living stone (1 Pet 2:5; John 1:42), he must have known exactly what I was like, yet he still made the promise. And what was it he said? "When you have recovered, strengthen your brethren." So Christ not only knew I should fall, but he wanted me to know beforehand that he would see me through and back again. He wanted me to know he still had use for me and a future.'

Final victory

And so Peter came back. Christ's prayer had prevailed. It was not for nothing that Christ had made a covenant in his own blood to write his laws on Peter's heart and turn Peter into a true and loyal man of

God. Nor had the interlude of his failure been without its part to play in the process of making him and, through him, untold numbers of other people holy. 'And when you have turned again, strengthen your brothers,' said Christ (Luke 22:32).

Peter remembered the charge; and in his first letter he set out to do just that. He tells his fellow Christians that their faith is like gold, incalculably precious; but like gold, at the beginning it is all mixed up with dross of one kind and another. It may be excitement or self-confidence and pride, second-hand experience or even childish father-fixations, and so it has to be purified. Like a goldsmith purifies his gold by putting it into the crucible and subjecting it to intense heat, so from time to time God must allow Christians to pass through suffering of various kinds.

Peter tells them not to be surprised when the fiery trial comes, as though something strange were happening to them. Their faith shall eventually result in praise and glory and honour at the revelation of Jesus Christ (1 Pet 4:12; 1:6–9). Where did Peter's confidence come from? It came first from the word and intercession of Christ, and then from his own experience. Anyone knows that, though a goldsmith may put his gold through the fire until it reaches melting point and beyond, he never allows any of the real gold to be destroyed. All he's getting rid of is the dross.

The royal outlaw

There was one more thing Christ had to say to his apostles before they left the upper room and went out to face Gethsemane and the cross. He had to make the implications of what was about to happen clear to them, or at least as clear as was possible at that moment. As the king himself, he was about to be declared an outlaw. It was nothing to be surprised at: the prophets had long since foretold it. But from now on it would mean a complete change for the apostles in the way they should conduct their mission in and to the world. When on previous occasions Christ had sent them to the Jewish nation to preach the gospel and announce the arrival of the king, Christ had expected the Jews to pay the day-to-day expenses of his apostles. He had a right to it. As their Messiah and liege lord, he had a sovereign's right to commandeer all he or his servants needed.

But now he was to be declared an outlaw, and to be executed. He would not resist or attempt to fight back and claim his rights. Therefore in the future his disciples and apostles could not expect the nation to maintain them, pay their salaries and provide the money for their missionary work or church buildings. They would have to pay their own way and fight their own battles. 'If anyone has no sword,' said Christ, 'let him sell his cloak and buy one.' 'Look, Lord,' said the apostles, 'here are two swords'—as if the Lord had meant it literally! Even if he had, two swords would have been pitifully inadequate to meet the opposition.

Later they were to see that clearly enough. As Paul put it, 'the weapons of our warfare are not of the flesh' (2 Cor 10:4). But just now their minds were full of new and amazing things. They were excited, and perhaps more than a little apprehensive. The hour was getting late too, and they would need all the strength they could muster to face the strain of the hours ahead. So they hadn't fully grasped the real nature of the fight before them; nor had they begun yet to understand what the king must now face. When it came to the battle they would fall asleep, and in the end desert him. He would have to fight alone, unsupported even by the fellowship of their prayers.

But the battle would be won, and already he could see them not as they were but as they would be when all the promises of his covenant had been fulfilled. The joy of it lit up his heart. But right now the covenant had not yet been signed, and the king must sign it in his own blood. Unless he died, the covenant would not be valid. 'All right', he said, as they stood there offering him their swords, ready at any cost to prevent him from dying, or so they thought. 'All right, you haven't understood quite yet, but you will. Come, let's go.'

The Gospel *for the* Doubter *and the* Skeptic

Inasmuch as many have undertaken to compile a narrative of the things that have been accomplished among us, just as those who from the beginning were eyewitnesses and ministers of the word have delivered them to us, it seemed good to me also, having followed all things closely for some time past, to write an orderly account for you, most excellent Theophilus, that you may have certainty concerning the things you have been taught.

In the days of Herod, king of Judea, there was a priest named Zechariah, of the division of Abijah. And he had a wife from the daughters of Aaron, and her name was Elizabeth. And they were both righteous before God, walking blamelessly in all the commandments and statutes of the Lord. But they had no child, because Elizabeth was barren, and both were advanced in years.

Now while he was serving as priest before God when his division was on duty, according to the custom of the priesthood, he was chosen by lot to enter the temple of the Lord and burn incense. And the whole multitude of the people were praying outside at the hour of incense.

And there appeared to him an angel of the Lord standing on the right side of the altar of incense. And Zechariah was troubled when he saw him, and fear fell upon him. But the angel said to him, 'Do not be afraid, Zechariah, for your prayer has been heard, and your wife Elizabeth will bear you a son, and you shall call his name John. And you will have joy and gladness, and many will rejoice at his birth, for he will be great before the Lord. And he must not drink wine or strong drink, and he will be filled with the Holy Spirit, even from his mother's womb. And he will turn many of the children of Israel to the Lord their God, and he will go before him in the spirit and power of Elijah, to turn the hearts of the fathers to the children, and the disobedient to the wisdom of the just, to make ready for the Lord a people prepared.'

And Zechariah said to the angel, 'How shall I know this? For I am an old man, and my wife is advanced in years.'

And the angel answered him, 'I am Gabriel. I stand in the

presence of God, and I was sent to speak to you and to bring you this good news. And behold, you will be silent and unable to speak until the day that these things take place, because you did not believe my words, which will be fulfilled in their time.'

And the people were waiting for Zechariah, and they were wondering at his delay in the temple. And when he came out, he was unable to speak to them, and they realized that he had seen a vision in the temple. And he kept making signs to them and remained mute. And when his time of service was ended, he went to his home.

After these days his wife Elizabeth conceived, and for five months she kept herself hidden, saying, 'Thus the Lord has done for me in the days when he looked on me, to take away my reproach among people.'

In the sixth month the angel Gabriel was sent from God to a city of Galilee named Nazareth, to a virgin betrothed to a man whose name was Joseph, of the house of David. And the virgin's name was Mary. And he came to her and said, 'Greetings, O favoured one, the Lord is with you!'

But she was greatly troubled at the saying, and tried to discern what sort of greeting this might be. And the angel said to her, 'Do not be afraid, Mary, for you have found favour with God. And behold, you will conceive in your womb and bear a son, and you shall call his name Jesus. He will be great and will be called the Son of the Most High. And the Lord God will give to him the throne of his father David, and he will reign over the house of Jacob for ever, and of his kingdom there will be no end.'

And Mary said to the angel, 'How will this be, since I am a virgin?'

And the angel answered her, 'The Holy Spirit will come upon you, and the power of the Most High will overshadow you; therefore the child to be born will be called holy—the Son of God. And behold, your relative Elizabeth in her old age has also conceived a son, and this is the sixth month with her who was called barren. For nothing will be impossible with God.'

And Mary said, 'Behold, I am the servant of the Lord; let it be to me according to your word.' And the angel departed from her.

In those days Mary arose and went with haste into the hill country, to a town in Judah, and she entered the house of Zechariah and greeted Elizabeth. And when Elizabeth heard the greeting of Mary, the baby leaped in her womb. And Elizabeth was filled with the Holy Spirit, and she exclaimed with a loud cry, 'Blessed are you among women, and blessed is the fruit of your womb! And why is this granted to me that the mother of my Lord should come to me? For behold, when the sound of your greeting came to my ears, the baby in my womb leaped for joy. And blessed is she who believed that there would be a fulfilment of what was spoken to her from the Lord.'

And Mary said,

'My soul magnifies the Lord, and my spirit rejoices in God my Saviour, for he has looked on the humble estate of his servant. For behold, from now on all generations will call me blessed; for he who is mighty has done great things for me, and holy is his name. And his mercy is for those who fear him from generation to generation. He has shown strength with his arm; he has scattered the proud in the thoughts of their hearts; he has brought down the mighty from their thrones and exalted those of humble estate; he has filled the hungry with good things, and the rich he has sent away empty. He has helped his servant Israel, in remembrance of his mercy, as he spoke to our fathers, to Abraham and to his offspring for ever.'

And Mary remained with her about three months and returned to her home.

Luke 1:1–56

We will bring our series of studies to an end by returning to the beginning of Luke's Gospel. Here we discover it is not only moderns who struggle to believe in miracles, nor is it the case that those who do believe do so because they do not understand the workings of natural processes. Indeed, Luke's infancy narratives concerning the Lord Jesus indicate that some who counted themselves believers in God were the very ones who were not prepared to believe all that God said at the time of Christ's birth. Still others listened and then obeyed, even at great personal cost.

At the beginning of his account, Luke indicates that he has listened to those who witnessed these events and compared the statements in order to present the evidence to those who are willing to consider it for themselves. Such a person was Theophilus, to whom Luke addresses his Gospel (1:1–4). Whether we are believers or unbelievers, cynical doubters or intrigued sceptics, Luke invites us all to consider what happened one night on a quiet Judaean hillside.

The infancy narratives and the struggle to believe

For many people, the thought of a shepherd and his sheep arouses pleasant and powerful feelings. The bleating of the innocent lambs and the defencelessness of the ewes appeal strongly to their protective instinct, which in turn identifies itself with the figure of the shepherd tending his sheep with loving care and guarding them with heroic devotion. The scene that Luke depicts outside Bethlehem, therefore, has immense appeal: a velvety dark sky overhead and shepherds lying out in the fields watching over their flocks, looking up at the brilliant but silent stars; the occasional bleating of the lambs, the quiet contentment of the ewes secure in their awareness of the shepherd's presence. Suddenly there is a burst of glory, and from the world above a great company of angels, full of praise and joyfulness, announcing the coming of one who would be a Saviour and protector for men, as the shepherds were for their sheep. Undeniably the story is attractive; but is it true?

To get a good look at the question, we ought first to take a more realistic look at the shepherds and their sheep. Sheep farming then as now was a smelly affair, involving the shepherd in long hours, tiresome work, and sometimes serious danger. On this particular night the shepherds were out in the fields, not for the sheer love of watching over sheep by night, but because they couldn't trust their fellow men not to steal them if they didn't watch over them; and also to stop wild beasts attacking and mauling the sheep. They could not afford to let robbers or beasts kill their sheep: they wanted eventually to kill the sheep themselves for meat, or sell them to someone else for the same purpose. When one thinks about it, their constant struggle against human crime and beastly savagery, the competition for pasture and the fight against disease are not altogether untypical of a good deal of human life.

It all serves to point the question the more sharply: Is Luke's story about angels factually true? Is there really a deathless glorious world beyond this one that is interested in our world and concerned to save us? Or is Luke's story nothing more than another example of the way we constantly try to disguise the unpleasant realities of cruelty and death that surround our lives by casting a poetic sentimental charm over them?

Sentimental imagination?

The feelings we have over shepherds and their sheep are not altogether false. Even though the shepherd may one day butcher his sheep, his care for them is real enough while it lasts. Certainly the shepherd and his care are not imaginary non-realities wishfully thought up by the sheep as a form of self-comfort to help them face frighteningly real wolves. But angels and heaven and a divine Saviour, such as Luke depicts, what are they? Have they objective reality like the shepherd and his care? Or are they simply subjective imaginations with which the early Christians tried to fill their minds to act as a buffer against the ugly realities of life? And all those other miraculous stories surrounding the birth of Christ—are they true? Literally and factually true? Atheists of course disbelieve them, but curiously enough not only atheists.

Pre-scientific myths?

Some who profess to accept the deity of Christ maintain that they cannot bring themselves to believe in the miraculous element in these stories. Wishing however to maintain their faith in Christ as the Son of God, and yet unable to accept the birth stories as literally true, they try to escape from their dilemma in various ways. Some say that the stories are beautifully imaginative and pious, but not literally and historically true. They were invented by the early Christians, who were convinced by the resurrection that Jesus was the Son of God and expressed their faith in his greatness and glory by inventing these imaginary stories and attaching them as a kind of halo round the record of his birth.

Others try a more sophisticated explanation. They hold that the stories contain a kernel of important truth, but the early Christians wrapped it in the language of myth, the detailed framework of which was their pre-scientific view of the universe. These early Christians are supposed to have believed in a three-decker universe, with heaven up above, hell down below and earth in the middle. In the course of telling their myths they happily talked of angels coming down from heaven and going back up again, whereas with our scientific attitude we cannot possibly accept these details as literally true. We know that the earth is round and that hell is not a little below Antarctica. We then are supposed to discard the outer wrappings of the myth and extract the inner kernel of truth—a delicate enough task when no one can tell us exactly where the wrapping ends and the kernel begins.

Unfortunately for this particular explanation of things, the early Christians who related these stories assure us that they knew what myths were, and that in presenting us with these stories they were not offering us myths. 'We did not follow cleverly devised myths', protests Peter (2 Pet 1:16).

Moreover, Luke, who actually wrote these stories, knew as well as we do that the earth is round. The Greeks had long since demonstrated that. Eratosthenes (276–194 BC) had arrived at a fairly accurate figure for the circumference of the earth, and Hipparchus (190–120 BC) had measured fairly accurately the distance of the moon. In the light of these and other astronomical discoveries by the Greeks, Julius Caesar had officially reformed the calendar used in the Roman Empire. There is not the slightest evidence that Luke, an educated and much travelled man, believed in a three-decker universe.

This would-be explanation founders on its own misconceptions in common with the one cited earlier. However, it is seized upon and held by people who imagine, quite sincerely, that it is their rational scientific outlook that makes it impossible for them to accept these birth stories literally. In view of this, Luke's first story is interesting. It will show us that it is neither science nor reason that makes it impossible for them to believe these miraculous stories, but something more like irrational instinct.

Zechariah and the agony of unbelief

The first miraculous event connected with the coming of Christ was the birth of John the Baptist to elderly parents; and the first man to disbelieve the story was the very first man to whom it was announced, namely John's father, Zechariah. Moreover he was not an atheist, nor even an agnostic, but a priest, a cleric in Jewish holy orders. For his unbelief, we are told, he was struck dumb. At least he was no credulous pre-scientific simpleton; he evidently knew enough about physical laws to consider the promised 'miracle' impossible. So let us examine Zechariah and see what kind of man he was, what his presuppositions were, and why the proposed miracle seemed incredible to him. We shall then be in a position to estimate how rational his unbelief was.

Zechariah was a priest, which presupposes a belief on his part in the existence of God. It is unlikely that Zechariah had ever envisaged atheism as a possible alternative creed. But if he had been faced with the choice between belief in a Creator and atheism, there is no denying that belief in a Creator would have been the more rational choice, since the existence of a Creator is the only grounds on which one can regard reason as ultimately valid. Atheism for its part requires us to believe that mind and reason arose by accident out of mindless matter, and that logic is the accidental and therefore ultimately meaningless product of a long chain of mindless accidents.

Zechariah moreover believed in angels—at least he seems not to have been particularly surprised when one visited him. But then it would have been remarkably small-minded and conceited of him to have believed, as some moderns seem to, that mankind is the highest form of intelligent life in all the vast universe.

Furthermore, Zechariah believed in prayer; and, granted only the existence of God, this belief too was reasonable. If we owe our faculty of love and our disposition to help others in need to a Creator God, it would hardly be reasonable to suppose that the Creator himself was loveless and indifferent to our need.

Zechariah believed in prayer, and for some years he had asked God to give him and his wife a son. In more recent years, however, he had left off praying that prayer. It seemed reasonable to pray for a child when both he and his wife were young enough to have one. At that stage he felt it was within the possibilities of nature that the mechanisms of Elizabeth's body could be nudged out of their inactivity into action. But now both of them were old and decrepit, and to have a child at this time of life would mean reversing the natural processes of ageing and recreating all the mechanisms of life. It was ludicrous, he felt, and quite irrational to expect any such thing, and impossible that it should happen.

And so, when the angel told him that his prayer of some years back was going to be answered, he was not prepared to believe it. He told Gabriel in fact that it would take much more than the bare word of an angel to convince him that such a miracle was possible. When the angel had delivered the message, Zechariah replied, 'How shall I know this?' (Luke 1:18). He said it politely, of course, but he meant it. He wasn't going to be dishonest and pretend he believed just because it was an angel who said it.

At this Gabriel struck him dumb. After all, it was impertinent to question the word of such an exalted messenger of God. But it was not only impertinent; it was stupid as well. He professed on the one hand to believe in a God who as Creator was the author and designer of all nature's processes; and yet on the other he was unable to believe that God could reverse the mechanisms he had himself created if he chose to, and renew the processes he had himself designed. It seems that God must content himself with working strictly within the processes he had designed, or forfeit credibility in Zechariah's eyes. Well, if that was how Zechariah felt, it was honest of him to say so; but he certainly had not been driven to this position of unbelief by some remorseless logic. His unbelief was anything but rational. It seems that the sudden announcement by the angel had found the unguarded weak point not only in his faith but in his rationality as well; it had penetrated through to the unbelief that is instinctive in fallen human nature.

Impossible or improbable?

But perhaps we are being a little unfair to Zechariah. Could it be that his difficulty was not that he thought the miracle was absolutely impossible, but only that it was improbable that such a miracle should happen to him? After all, miracles are by definition exceedingly rare occurrences, and it is the improbability of them happening on any given occasion to a particular person that bothers most people, rather than any outright impossibility.

But then the angel had carefully prepared Zechariah by explaining what the context of this miracle should be: it was to be done, not to gratify Zechariah's ambitions or even to foster his private devotional life, but to herald an event as unique as the creation itself—the entry into his created world of the Creator incarnate. The Old Testament Scriptures, which Zechariah knew and professed to hold as the word of God, plainly indicated that this august event should be preceded and prepared for by a totally remarkable and unique prophetic witness; and in making his announcement the angel had specifically called Zechariah's attention to these prophecies.

Had Zechariah protested to the angel that it was incredible that he and his wife should be chosen to play even a minor part in this great event, we might well have applauded his pious humility—though unbelief in the word of an angel does not fit well with piety. When he replied to the angel's announcement, it was not the unlikelihood that he should be chosen for such high office that was preoccupying Zechariah, but simply the physical impossibility, as he regarded it, of the angel's words coming true. 'How shall I know this?' he protested. 'For I am an old man, and my wife is advanced in years' (1:18). For expressing unbelief on those grounds he was rightly struck dumb.

On this day when the angel appeared to Zechariah in the temple, he was not saying prayers for his own personal needs only. The whole multitude of the people were praying outside the temple while Zechariah was supposedly representing them inside. In their simplicity they probably never dreamed that at the heart of their professional priest, there nestled an unbelief that made a mockery of prayer. If God is limited to doing only those things that the normal course of nature could and would do anyway, what is the point of asking God to do anything? To ask him to interfere in the normal working of nature, and do something that nature left to herself would not or could not do, is to ask him to do a miracle. But why ask him, if you do not believe he can do miracles?

Appropriately the angel struck Zechariah dumb—that was the end of him saying public prayers for the time being. Moreover, when he went outside to bless the people who were waiting for him, he could not speak to them. But then a priest who cannot believe in miracles has no message for the people anyway, and certainly no gospel. If God cannot restore the body of one elderly woman, what hope would there be that he could restore the whole universe? If God could not give new life to a body decrepit but still living, how could he raise from the tomb a body three days dead? And if Christ has not been raised from the dead there is no gospel to preach and the future holds nothing but the dumb unbreakable silence of a universal grave.

The virgin birth and obstacles to faith

Now compare the angel's response to the similar questions asked in Luke 1. When Gabriel told Zechariah that he and his wife were going to have a son, Zechariah replied, 'How shall I know this?' (1:18), and he was struck dumb. When Gabriel told Mary that she was to bear a child, she replied, 'How will this be?' (1:34), and she was not struck dumb. The reason is obvious: her question, though superficially similar to Zechariah's, was in fact quite different and sprang from a very different attitude. Zechariah doubted the angel's word, and therefore asked how he could know it was true. Mary believed the angel's word, and simply asked by what means it should be fulfilled. Zechariah was preoccupied with the physical difficulty: he and his wife were old, so how could they have a child? Mary's difficulty too was in a sense physical, but much more predominantly moral: 'I am not married,' she said, 'how then shall I have a child?' To have a child out of wedlock was to her unthinkable, not because it would require a miracle, for it wouldn't; but because the only way known to her of it happening would be immoral.

Was the angel's announcement virtually a command to get married? She was, after all, already betrothed to Joseph, so what was more natural than that she might now be expected to hasten the time of her marriage? Gabriel's answer must have stunned her. When he had first greeted her, she had been greatly troubled at the wording of his salutation, and his subsequent prophecy of the greatness of her child can only have increased her wonder. But it must have overwhelmed her to now be told that she was to conceive a child before marriage by the direct intervention of the Holy Spirit. On the one hand, there was the immeasurably exalted privilege of being chosen to be the vehicle of the incarnation; but at the same time there was the agonizing prospect of being disbelieved, even by her closest friends, and having to live under a cloud of suspicion.

Her immediate meek response, 'Behold, I am the servant of the Lord; let it be to me according to your word' (Luke 1:38), shows the wealth of divine grace that was given her. But we have no need on that account to imagine that Mary was anything less than a realist. In her Jewish community, for a betrothed girl to become pregnant before marriage by someone other than her husband-to-be was regarded not as youthful impatience but as downright adultery. We know what our own reaction would be to a girl in this state who tried to explain her condition by a story of angelic visitation and divine intervention! What is more relevant, we know from Matthew's account exactly what her husband-to-be thought of her story: much as he loved her, he found it quite unacceptable.

Some people talk as if the early Christians were ready in their religious zeal to believe any old story so long as it was liberally embellished with the pious and miraculous. They forget, if ever they did know it, that among religious people it is the poor and uneducated who tend to take the moral demands of their religion seriously. They are used to accepting the authority of the law without question, and they have not acquired the sophistication with which the rich and educated excuse or even justify their aberrations.

Joseph was a peasant carpenter and a devout man; he not only totally disbelieved Mary's story but he 'resolved to divorce her quietly' (Matt 1:19), that is, to break off the betrothal and refuse to marry her.

Mary must have foreseen it. The moment Gabriel made the announcement, instinct would have flashed before her mind the kind of reception she was bound to get. And that not only from Joseph but from the public at large. And certainly that instinct proved true. Later, in our Lord's public ministry, his opponents were still taunting him with having been born out of wedlock. 'We were not born of sexual immorality', they said (John 8:41).

The resurrection

If Joseph initially disbelieved her story, what evidence is there to make us think that it is true? There is overwhelming evidence. For us, the resurrection of Mary's son from the dead puts her account of his conception beyond all doubt. It is impossible to believe in the resurrection of Christ and not accept his deity. And it would be absurd to accept his deity and yet hold that the woman through whom deity chose to effect the incarnation could have been mistaken in her story of how that divine event took place. And it is utterly unthinkable that she should have deliberately put about a fiction of her own imagination.

Now, when it comes to a question of the evidence for the deity of Christ, the apostles in their public preaching always cite the resurrection above all else, and they offer themselves as eyewitnesses whose evidence can be scrutinized and cross-examined. They do not cite the virgin birth as evidence; not because they do not believe it, as some have naively suggested, but because it would hardly have been appropriate to publicly cross-examine Mary, the only witness of its happening, on such an intimate matter. Though it is Mary, of course, who was the source of the accounts that we have, as we shall consider presently. We who have come to faith through the witness of the apostles believe in the virgin birth because we first believe in the resurrection and deity of Christ; we do not believe in the deity of Christ because we first believe in the virgin birth.

Incidentally, while we are considering the witness of the apostles, it will be convenient to consider an objection against the historicity of the virgin birth that is sometimes made on the grounds of an expression used by Paul in Galatians 4. He describes Christ as 'born of woman' (v. 4); and some people claim this shows that Paul considered there was nothing extraordinary about the birth of Christ, but rather that he was born of woman just like any other man; and they conclude therefore that Paul did not believe in the virgin birth.

We may grant their premise, though we reject their conclusion. The miraculous element in the way in which our Lord entered into our world was not, strictly speaking, in his birth, but in his conception. The birth presumably took place according to the ordinary natural processes. Nor is this splitting hairs. When Paul insists that Christ's birth was like any other man's birth ('of woman') he is intending to make the point that Christ's appearance in our world was not a theophany or a phantasm; it was a real incarnation. He is not intending to deny, even by implication, that the conception was miraculous. It is manifestly false logic to suppose that the premise 'ordinary birth' demands the conclusion 'ordinary conception'.

A real man

But at this point we meet a much more serious objection. There are those who contend that the theology of the rest of the New Testament makes it impossible for us to believe in the virgin birth. They point out that the New Testament elsewhere stresses the fact that Christ was a real man: 'he had to be made like his brothers in every respect' (Heb 2:17); and they argue that if Christ's birth was in any way special or miraculous, then Christ would not be man in the identical sense that we are; and this, they urge, would be a denial of his true humanity and thus a serious heresy.

It is a sufficient answer to this objection to point out that Paul himself, in a very famous passage, argues at length that Christ, though truly human, was a different kind of man from Adam—even from what Adam was in his unfallen state. 'Thus it is written, "The first man Adam became a living being"; the last Adam became a life-giving spirit' (1 Cor 15:45). This is no place to try and explain what the New Testament itself does not try to explain, namely how Christ could be both God and man; but it is true to say that while the New Testament asserts that Christ was truly man, it nowhere asserts that he was only man. So then, the account of the miraculous conception does not conflict with the New Testament statement of the true humanity of Christ.

A detailed account

But to return now to Luke's account of the virgin birth. To say that we believe it primarily because we first believe in the resurrection and deity of Christ, does not mean that the story of the virgin birth is itself simply a poetical expression of the church's faith in the greatness of Christ and not a literal historical event. Consider, for instance, the circumstantial detail given in the story:

> After these days his wife Elizabeth conceived, and for five
> months she kept herself hidden ... In the sixth month the angel
> Gabriel was sent ... to a virgin ... And behold, your relative
> Elizabeth ... has also conceived ... and this is the sixth month
> with her ... In those days Mary arose ... and she entered the
> house of ... Elizabeth ... And Mary remained with her about
> three months and returned to her home. Now the time came for
> Elizabeth to give birth. (Luke 1:24–57)

Detailed mention of the timing of the various stages in a story is very
natural in any account given by someone who was a principal actor in
the events described. In moments of heightened emotion, details of
time and place imprint themselves indelibly on the mind of the person
who is undergoing whatever experience it is, and they tend to get
repeated whenever the story is told. But more: when it comes to the
conception and birth of her children, the one thing a mother would
notice instinctively and remember above all else is the time of events.

Luke states in his preface (1:1–2) that his narrative is based on
eyewitness accounts, which must mean he is claiming that the story of
the virgin birth comes ultimately from Mary herself. If this is basically
Mary's story, such detail of the timings is just what we might expect;
whereas were it merely a poetic way of saying that Christ was a special
person, such exact circumstantial detail would not be needed, and we
should not expect it.

On the other hand, consider the implications if the story is not
historical but only some kind of myth, as some say. Luke makes a great
point of claiming that his stories are taken from eyewitness accounts.
If then, having made this claim so vigorously, his very first story is not
taken from an eyewitness account but is a myth, Luke is at once con-
victed of the most serious misrepresentation. In addition, if he has gone
out of his way to add circumstantial details of timing to make the myth
appear to be an historical event when it is not, no amount of scholarly
reasoning can relieve him of a charge of deliberate intent to deceive.

More evidence

The details of timing however not only point to Mary as the source
of the story, but they offer indirect evidence of its truthfulness. We

are told that Mary stayed with Elizabeth about three months before the birth of Elizabeth's child. Three months in this context must at the very least mean nearer three months than two, and Elizabeth was already in her sixth month of pregnancy when Gabriel appeared to Mary. This shows us that Mary must have gone to see Elizabeth and must have told her about the angel's announcement immediately after it had been made, and before she could have had definite physical evidence that she was going to have a child. Had she waited until the physical evidence forced her to attempt some explanation of what she could no longer hide, suspicion might well have been cast on her story.

When Semele in Greek legend gave birth to a child before marriage, her parents, so Euripides tells us (Bacchae 26–42, 333–334) made up and put about the story that Semele had been visited by a god. It was done to save the family's name, though of course her sisters never did believe the story.

But there is nothing like this about Mary's story. The evidence lies before us that she did not invent the story after the physical evidence of pregnancy compelled her to attempt some explanation; and that being so, it is impossible to imagine any reason why she should invent it at all. She told what she told simply because it happened.

The mention of Semele and the ancient world of myth suggests that here perhaps is the place to deal with another popular objection to the historicity of the virgin birth. It is an objection levelled by the pseudo-learned who have become aware that the ancient pagan mythologies are full of stories of virgins who are supposed to have had children by deities and demigods. On the strength of this they jump to the conclusion that the virgin birth is but one more mythical story of this kind, and they suppose that the early Christians would have credited it because they lived in a world which popular imagination had peopled with multitudes of gods and goddesses.

They seem to have overlooked the fact that the first Christians were Jews, who were strict monotheists even though they lived in a pagan world. According to their beliefs, the only superhuman beings capable of intercourse with human women would be evil spirits (see Gen 6:4; Jude 6–7). Moreover, though Luke was a Gentile, in his writings he denounced the crude follies of polytheistic paganism as strongly as any Jew (see Acts 14:11–18). It is a gross absurdity therefore, to suggest that the story of the virgin birth as related by the early

Christians had the slightest connection whatever with the polytheistic myths current in the pagan world of their time.

Old Testament prophecy

Much more serious is an objection frequently urged by modern scholars against the historicity of the virgin birth. They maintain that the genesis of the story was as follows. In the Greek translation of the prophet Isaiah the early Christians found a prophecy that a virgin should conceive and bear a son. And because they believed that every Old Testament prophecy, which could with any degree of plausibility be applied to the Messiah, must have been fulfilled in the life of Jesus Christ, they invented the story of the virgin birth to make it appear that he had fulfilled this prophecy too. And for good measure these scholars generally add that the Christians who did this work of invention are caught red-handed because the word 'virgin' in the Greek version is a mistranslation of the original Hebrew, which indicates not a virgin but simply a young woman.

We will pass over the deliberate misrepresentation of the facts that this explanation imputes to the early Christians, however well motivated they may have been; though it is a serious matter that no scholarly reasoning can adequately justify. It brings us to two pertinent considerations.

Firstly, if the whole point of inventing the story lay in demonstrating that Jesus fulfilled Isaiah's prophecy, how does it come that Luke manages to tell the whole story in great detail without ever once mentioning the prophecy? Secondly, Matthew, who is the only New Testament writer to mention the prophecy, gives the sequence of events as follows. Joseph first heard of the idea of a virgin birth when he was confronted with the girl whom he intended to marry and to whom he was betrothed, pregnant by someone else. She tried to tell him that this was a supernatural virginal conception, but he rejected the whole story as utterly incredible and decided to break off the engagement. But an angel appeared to him and assured him that the whole thing really was a miracle from God. And only subsequently would Joseph or the early Christians find confirmation of the angel's message in an Old Testament prophecy about a virgin birth. Joseph would never have rejected Mary's story so completely and decidedly, and intended to put her away, if he had known of this prophecy from the start, and if he had been expecting its fulfilment.

So then, if Matthew's critics are right, Matthew has not only concocted an imaginary story and palmed it off as though it were genuine history in order to make the bogus point that the birth of Jesus fulfilled the prophecy of a virginal conception. Like an expert thief, he has tried to cover up his tracks and mislead his readers as to the real origin of his story by making out that neither Joseph nor the early Christians were aware of the prophecy until after the virginal conception had taken place. To imply that an apostle is a deliberate deceiver is a heavy price to pay in order to escape the necessity of believing in the miracle of the virgin birth.

And now, as if we have not already had enough of strange views, we must consider one more attempt to bypass a literal acceptance of the virgin birth. Some remind us that the Jewish rabbis used to say, 'There are three partners in [the production of] man, the Holy One, blessed be He, his father and his mother' (see Niddah 31a). We are then asked to believe that when the early Christians claimed that Christ was conceived of the Holy Spirit, they did not intend to say anything more than what these rabbis said; but unfortunately later Christians misunderstood and thought they meant that Mary's child had a divine Father but not a human father.

So on this view the whole story of the miraculous birth of Christ can and should be boiled down to a claim, made apparently with great vigour by the early Christians, that the birth of Christ had nothing special or remarkable about it beyond what could be said of any other man's birth. One is left wondering why they ever bothered to make the claim. If unbelief in miracles has to bring itself to such contorted explanations in order to explain away the story of the virgin birth, then all one can say is that intellectually unbelief is harder than faith.

More to find in Luke's Gospel

Though we now must draw our studies to a close, your enjoyment of this Gospel need not end; it is there for you to continue reading. We have looked at some of what Luke has compiled, but there is of course much that we have not considered. His account will continue to bring certainty to those who read it, which was the intention in the first place (Luke 1:4).

The many other scenes that he has chosen show more of the wonder of the good news that Christ brought to the needy—a gospel of forgiveness and hope. As you continue to read, may you see Christ not only in those historical scenes but also as the one who died and is risen again. And may we all, like the two travellers on the road to Emmaus (24:13), come to know Jesus Christ, and so to love and worship him as our Lord.

Study Guidelines *for* Leaders

Study Guide

These questions are intended for personal or group study. Individuals who use them are likely to find it helpful to refer to the questions as they come to each chapter, though some may wish to wait until they have read the entire book and then use the questions to review the material. For Bible classes, seminars and home study groups, the following guidelines are offered as a suggested use of the questions:

1. Allow 45 minutes for discussion.
2. Read the questions briefly before you read the lesson in order to make yourself or your group familiar with the central issues discussed.
3. Read the Bible passages on which the lesson is based.
4. Read the lesson.
5. Consider the questions in turn. In a group situation, the leader should ensure that each question is dealt with and that the discussion remains relevant.
6. It may be useful in a group situation at the beginning of the session to assign a question to one or more members of the group. This person or persons will then have the responsibility of leading that section of the discussion; the leader will ensure that time is efficiently allocated so that all questions are dealt with. The Holy Spirit calls us to be grown-ups in intellect and to use that intellect diligently as we come to the Scriptures (1 Cor 14:20). Yet we do not study unaided; our Lord himself opens his disciples' minds so that they might understand the Scriptures (Luke 24:45).

Panorama 1: The Gospel of the Outcast and Oppressed

Scene 1: Reclaiming a Prostitute

1. What sort of person does Christ appear to be from this passage?
2. Why was Christ not interested in Simon's good works and self-righteousness?

3. How do we know that the woman had been forgiven?
4. What does this story tell us about what a sinner is?
5. What is Christ's attitude to our sin? Does he offer forgiveness to us today?

Scene 2: Redeeming a Swindler

1. Who are the 'decent' people, then and now?
2. What was the result of Levi's response to Christ?
3. Who needed Christ more, the Pharisees or the tax collectors? Why did he go to the tax collectors?
4. What is the parable of the Pharisee and the tax collector saying about good works?
5. What is the difference between rewards for work done in this life, and salvation?
6. What did Christ say to Zacchaeus that changed his life in a way that years of preaching had failed to do?

Scene 3: Avenging the Widow

1. Why does God seem to allow evil to go unchecked?
2. What do we mean when we say that Christ came to liberate the oppressors as well as the oppressed?
3. Is there a sense in which we are all oppressors?
4. What is the main lesson of the story about the Sidonian widow?
5. Why did Christ's listeners put him out of the synagogue?
6. What aspects of this story apply to modern life?

Scene 4: Converting a Criminal

1. Why did one criminal call on Christ for forgiveness while the other cursed him?
2. How was Christ different from the other kings that the dying thief would have known about?
3. How did faith in Christ differ from 'religion' for the dying thief?

4. What do we learn about repentance from this story?
5. In what ways may we submit to Christ's authority today?
6. Can Christ claim my loyalty today? On what basis?

Panorama 1: Suggestions for Further Study

In Panorama 1 we dealt with four cases of socially outcast or under-privileged people. Luke's Gospel presents us with others as well. Here are some examples with the references in the Gospel and suggested background reading.

Victims of disease

> Lepers: Luke 5:12–16; 17:11–19; 4:27
> Background: Leviticus 13

A victim of mental illness induced by spiritism

> The Demon Possessed Man: Luke 8:26–39
> Background: Leviticus 19:31; 20:6, 27; 17:7–8

Victims of religious feuds

> The Samaritans: Luke 9:51–56; 10:25–37; 17:15–19
> Background: 2 Kings 17; Nehemiah; John 4
> In each case:

1. Investigate the nature of the rejection, isolation and loneliness suffered.
2. Estimate how justified, if at all, society was in imposing the isolation, and/or why it was ineffectual in removing the cause.
3. Study, where appropriate, the effects not only upon the victims but upon society.
4. Pay special attention to the different methods Christ used to deal with these differing cases.

Panorama 2: The Gospel of the Here and the Hereafter

Scene 5: Centre-point of Time

1. Why do Christians claim that the death of Christ was the 'centre-point' of time?
2. Why, from God's point of view, was Christ's death necessary?
3. How did the death of Christ break the power of death (Heb 2:14–15)?
4. How may an individual today be sure of heaven?
5. What are the implications of Christ's death with regard to personal guilt and forgiveness?

Scene 6: Gateway to Eternity

1. What is the difference between being 'in Adam' and 'in Christ'?
2. Why is morality (the law of God) unable to provide forgiveness?
3. Why, from man's point of view, was Christ's death necessary?
4. Why do Christians claim that Jesus Christ is different from all other religious leaders?
5. What are the chief features of the coming kingdom of God?

Scene 7: When We Cross Over

1. What did Simeon and the dying thief have in common as they approached death?
2. On what basis may we be sure of heaven?
3. What is eternal life?
4. What does it mean to personally trust in the Lamb of God, in him and in nothing else; and to have our names written in his book of life?

Scene 8: Over on the Other Side

1. Why did the rich man go to hell?
2. What evidence have we that it is possible to go straight to be with Christ when we die?
3. What information does Luke provide concerning the future of the unbelieving and unrepentant?
4. How may we make sure that we have a good foundation for enjoying eternity?

Panorama 3: The Gospel of the King and His Present Kingdom

Scene 9: The King Announces His Covenant

1. What does one have to do to benefit from the new covenant?
2. Why was the old covenant impossible for humans to keep? What was its purpose?
3. Why is God not satisfied when we do our best and keep the commandments as well as we can?
4. Why was Christ's death necessary before the new covenant could be introduced?
5. How do Hebrews 8:8–12 and Galatians 3:15–22 explain the differences between the two covenants?

Scene 10: The Relationship Between the Sovereign and His Subjects

1. Why does God go to such lengths to assure the true Christian of complete acceptance?
2. What does God mean when he speaks of not remembering our sins? On what basis can he do this?
3. What, in your own words, are the three main clauses of the new covenant as set out in Hebrews 8:6–13?
4. Clause 2 speaks about knowing the Lord (v. 11). How may we know the Lord? (You may also wish to look at John 17:3.)
5. What is the significance of the death of Christ in making possible the new covenant (Heb 9:15)?

Scene 11: The Rank and Reward of the King's Servants

1. What rewards does Christ promise to the person who follows him and suffers with him?
2. When will these rewards be enjoyed and why is this important?
3. What do the examples of Peter and Paul teach us about the nature of Christian service and the style of life of those with Christian responsibility?
4. What do we learn from Christ's attitude to the blind man about his care for people in need?

Scene 12: The King–Priest and the Royal Outlaw

1. What lessons did Peter learn about himself through his experience of denial and Christ's forgiveness (see 1 Pet 1:6–9; 4:12)?
2. Why did Christ allow Peter to be tested?
3. Why is our faith so important? (Christ prayed particularly for Peter's faith.)
4. What evidence is there that Christ is interested in us as individuals and in our particular needs?

Conclusion

Chapter 13: The Gospel for the Doubter and the Sceptic

1. Why is it difficult for people to say that they believe in the deity of Christ, and yet deny the miraculous elements in Luke's infancy narratives?
2. What was the difference in the questions that Mary and Zechariah asked the angel, and how does that difference relate to our questions and our faith today?
3. According to the example of the apostles in the book of Acts, which is the better evidence for the deity of Christ: the virgin birth or the resurrection? Why so?
4. Do you find the specific objections raised against the virgin birth convincing, or are they adequately answered by the evidence given in both the Old Testament and the New?

Scripture Index

Scripture Index

Scripture Index

Scripture Index

Other Resources on Luke's Gospel

The resources listed below are free for you to read and/or listen to on our website (myrtlefieldhouse.com). New resources continue to be added as they become available to us. To stay up to date with these, join our email newsletter.

Myrtlefield Expositions

According to Luke
The Third Gospel's Ordered Historical Narrative

Myrtlefield Sermons

They Followed Jesus
Twelve Studies on Major Themes in Luke

Key New Testament Themes
Ten Studies Covering Matthew, Luke, Galatians and 1 John

True Emotion
One Study on Three Groups of Women and Their Tears

A Well-Balanced Mind
One Study from Luke on Faith and Works

What is Your Name?
One Study from Luke 8 on the Healing of the Possessed Man

Two Prepared Entries into Jerusalem
One Study from Luke 19 and 22 on the Lord's Supper

www.myrtlefieldhouse.com

Our website contains hundreds of resources in a variety of formats. You can read, listen to or watch David Gooding's teaching on over 35 Bible books and 14 topics. You can also view the full catalogue of Myrtlefield House publications and download free e-book editions of most of our books and all of our sermon transcripts. The website is optimized for both computer and mobile viewing, making it easy for you to access the resources at home or on the go.

For more information about any of our publications or resources contact us at: info@myrtlefieldhouse.com

Myrtlefield Expositions

Myrtlefield Expositions provide insights into the thought flow and meaning of the biblical writings, motivated by devotion to the Lord who reveals himself in the Scriptures. Scholarly, engaging, and accessible, each book addresses the reader's mind and heart to increase faith in God and to encourage obedience to his word. Teachers, preachers and all students of the Bible will find the approach to Scripture adopted in these volumes both instructive and enriching.

The Riches of Divine Wisdom
The New Testament's Use of the Old Testament

According to Luke
The Third Gospel's Ordered Historical Narrative

True to the Faith
The Acts of the Apostles: Defining and Defending the Gospel

In the School of Christ
Lessons on Holiness in John 13–17

An Unshakeable Kingdom
The Letter to the Hebrews for Today

Myrtlefield Encounters

Myrtlefield Encounters are complementary studies of biblical literature, Christian teaching and apologetics. The books in this series engage the minds of believers and sceptics. They show how God has spoken in the Bible to address the realities of life and its questions, problems, beauty and potential.

Key Bible Concepts
Defining the Basic Terms of the Christian Faith

Christianity: Opium or Truth?
Answering Thoughtful Objections to the Christian Faith

The Definition of Christianity
Exploring the Original Meaning of the Christian Faith

The Bible and Ethics
Finding the Moral Foundations of the Christian Faith

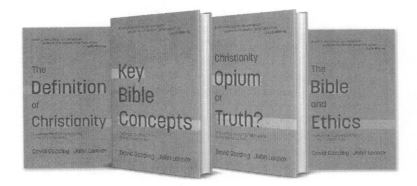

Bringing Us To Glory

Our lives are a mix of difficulties, laughter and delight, of satisfying moments, seemingly hopeless situations and unanswerable questions. Nature's beauty inspires our wonder today, but its power may break our bodies tomorrow. What will steady our faith in God, and help it to grow, when life is like that?

Far from wanting us to live in a make-believe world, the call of God's word is to see the reality of what God is doing in the lives of millions of people. Scripture tells us that, right now, he is working out his long-term plan for bringing many sons and daughters to full maturity in his Son, Jesus Christ. The more we understand the revelation of his plan, and the character of the one who has decided to bring us on a journey through this world of brokenness and beauty, the more we will be drawn to follow him in obedience, love and trust.

These 365 one-page readings focus on Christ's work as the captain of our salvation, on the way he journeys with his redeemed, and finally on the wisdom and love of the Father who planned it all.

> You will consider *Bringing Us To Glory* one of God's best gifts to your own devotional life. Read it, and reap! — *O. S. Hawkins*

> This book is equal to a full year at any theological college. I realize more than ever why so many of my friends have been mentored by Dr Gooding. — *George Verwer*

> It is clear we are reading a man who has fallen in love with the glory and majesty of God. This is a must read! — *Rebecca Manley Pippert*

Sample Reading from *Bringing Us To Glory*

15th April

CHRIST'S FUTURE GLORY

Reading: Luke 9:26–36

He received honour and glory from God the Father, and the voice was borne to him by the Majestic Glory, 'This is my beloved Son, with whom I am well pleased'. (2 Peter 1:17)

The conversation between Christ, Moses and Elijah was about Christ's exodus at Jerusalem, about the fact that he must leave the glory of the transfiguration mount, go down into the squalid sinful world below, on to Jerusalem and death: the Son of Man had to go even as it had been ordained. Moses and Elijah therefore were now already beginning to depart when Peter suggested that it would be good if they did not go, but all stayed where they were on the mountain. He proposed in fact to make three tents, one each for Christ, Moses and Elijah, to facilitate their stay. He, like the other two apostles, had been asleep, Luke says, and he did not realize what he was saying. It was nonetheless a most unfortunate suggestion. Not only did it imply putting Moses and Elijah on a level with Christ, but it would have impeded and delayed the very going which had been planned from eternity and for which the time had now come. It was at that point in the proceedings, when having discussed his exodus Moses and Elijah were departing and Christ was turning to go down the mountain and on to his exodus, that the cloud came and Jesus received from the 'Majestic Glory' himself the tremendous accolade of honour and glory: 'This is my Son, my Chosen One; hear him'. Not only had the exodus been planned by the Father: Christ's willingness to fulfil it filled the Father's heart with delight and moved him thus to honour the Son.

As Peter reflected on this glorious event in later life, it convinced him of two things. First, the death of Christ was no tragic accident: it was foreknown, that is foreordained, before the foundation of the world (see 1 Pet 1:20). Secondly, the shame and death of the cross were no obstacle in the way of Christ's setting up of the kingdom. His willingness to suffer was the reason for the Father's delight, the grounds for his bestowing on Jesus the supreme glory. Not only had he already raised him from the dead and given him glory: one day he would do before the whole universe what he had done on the mount of transfiguration. He would glorify and vindicate his Son: Christ would come again not only in his personal glory but in the glory of the Father himself and of the holy angels. No glory would be too great for the Father to bestow upon the one crucified.

Myrtlefield Discoveries

Myrtlefield Discoveries combine depth of insight with accessible style in order to help today's readers find the Bible's meaning and its significance for all of life. Covering whole books of the Bible, themes or topics, each book in this series serves as a guide to the wonders of God's word. The material is intended to prepare readers to share what they have learned. Study groups, teachers and individual students will all benefit from the way these books open up the biblical text and reveal its application for life.

Windows on Paradise
Scenes of Hope and Salvation in the Gospel of Luke

Journeys with Jesus
True Stories of Changed Destinies in John's Gospel

Drawing Near To God
Lessons From the Tabernacle for Today

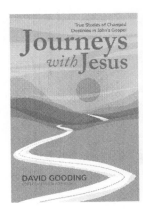

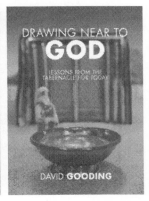